The Fast Forward MBA in Hiring

THE FAST FORWARD MBA SERIES

The Fast Forward MBA Series provides time-pressed business professionals and students with concise, one-stop information to help them solve business problems and make smart, informed business decisions. All of the volumes, written by industry leaders, contain "tough ideas made easy." The published books in this series are:

The Fast Forward MBA in Business
(0-471-14660-9)
by Virginia O'Brien

The Fast Forward MBA in Finance
(0-471-10930-4)
by John Tracy

The Fast Forward MBA Pocket Reference
(0-471-14595-5)
by Paul A. Argenti

The Fast Forward MBA in Marketing
(0-471-16616-2)
by Dallas Murphy

The Fast Forward MBA in Hiring

Finding and Keeping the Best People

MAX MESSMER

Chairman and CEO, Robert Half International Inc.

John Wiley & Sons, Inc.

New York • Chichester • Weinheim • Brisbane • Singapore • Toronto

This book is printed on acid-free paper. ♾

Published by John Wiley & Sons, Inc.
Published simultaneously in Canada.

Library of Congress Cataloging-in-Publication Data:
Messmer, Max, 1946–
The fast forward MBA in hiring : finding and keeping the best people / Max Messmer.
p. cm. — (The fast forward MBA series)
Includes index.
ISBN 0-471-24212-8 (pbk. : alk. paper)
1. Employees—Recruiting. 2. Employee selection.
I. Title. II. Series.
HF5549.5.R44M47 1998
658.3′11—dc21 97-35609
CIP

Printed in the United States of America.

10 9 8 7 6 5 4 3 2 1

Acknowledgment of copyrighted material can be found on page 229.

To my wife, Marcia, and my two sons, Michael and Matthew, for their love and support.

ABOUT THE AUTHOR

MAX MESSMER

Max Messmer is chairman and CEO of Robert Half International Inc., the world's largest specialized staffing firm. He is a widely recognized expert on careers and hiring, and is the author of three other critically acclaimed books: *Staffing Europe: An Indispensable Guide to Hiring and Being Hired in the New Europe; 50 Ways to Get Hired;* and, most recently, *Job Hunting For Dummies.* Messmer's job search expertise has been featured in *Fortune, Forbes, Time,* and *The Wall Street Journal,* as well as on CNN and other television venues. Messmer's company, which was founded in 1948 by Robert Half, has successfully placed hundreds of thousands of people in professional positions. Messmer lives in California.

ACKNOWLEDGMENTS

My sincerest thanks go out to those whose knowledge, commitment, and hard work made this book possible: Barry Tarshis and Colleen Rumsey for their voluminous research and insight; Lynn Taylor, vice president and director of research at Robert Half International, for her expertise and invaluable input; and members of Lynn's staff, including Reesa McCoy Staten and Laurel Goddard.

CONTENTS

INTRODUCTION

Everyone knows that, regardless of how big your business is and what industry you are in, you cannot hope to succeed in today's fast-paced, increasingly competitive business environment unless you have a workforce that is not only capable and productive, but highly motivated as well. The tight labor market in the 1990s, coupled with the rapidly growing importance of technology and major demographic changes, has put enormous pressure on companies to hire and retain employees who can meet the performance challenges that exist today.

This book has a simple but far-reaching objective: to provide you with cutting-edge information, ideas, and tools that will enhance your ability not only to hire the best possible people but to also help you develop an overall approach to staffing that is strategically keyed to the needs and goals of your business.

The notion of viewing hiring as a strategic process keyed to business goals (as opposed to simply "filling" jobs)—is often referred to as *strategic staffing,* and it represents the philosophical cornerstone of this book. It also sets this book apart from other books on the same subject—*The Fast Forward MBA in Hiring* is much more than a crash course in successful interviewing techniques.

Yes, we will be covering interviewing techniques in depth—and we will be describing for you the interviewing practices and techniques of today's most progressive companies. But the distinguishing characteristic of this book is that it deals with the *totality* of the hiring process. Indeed, it is the fundamental premise of this book that successful hiring practices are rooted in disciplined, strategic thinking through *every* phase of the process—and particularly in the beginning, when you first start to analyze your needs.

The book begins with an overview of the forces that have come together to create the need for bold new approaches to hiring—with special emphasis on how the very concept of *job* is undergoing dramatic change in today's workplace. In the two chapters that follow this overview, you'll get an in-depth look at two of the least understood and most often ignored aspects of hiring: (1) identifying your staffing needs and (2) exploring all the options that are open to you as you seek to meet those needs. Chief among the highlights of these two chapters is a four-step process designed to help you determine whether your current strategy is in sync with the demands of your business.

Chapters 4, 5, and 6 deal with recruiting, screening, and interviewing, respectively; in each chapter you will get an in-depth look at how today's most innovative companies are dealing with each of these essential components of the hiring process. Chapter 7 focuses on the hiring decision itself—and what you need to do to increase your chances of making the "right" decision. Chapter 8 guides you through the various steps you need to take once the hiring decision has been made. And Chapters 9 and 10 will give you new ideas on how to retain and get the most out of the high-performing employees you've just hired—and how to respond when the "best" candidate fails to live up to his or her potential.

We have done our very best to make this book up-to-date, accurate, and relevant to today's business environment, and we have gone out of our way to present information in a manner that will enable you to apply it directly and productively to the staffing challenges you face in your business.

The Fast Forward MBA in Hiring

CHAPTER 1

Shifting Tides—Strategic Hiring in the New Darwinian Marketplace

INTRODUCTION

The recruiting, hiring, and retaining of competent, hardworking, and reliable employees has always been a critical function in business, but managing this function effectively is far more complex today than ever before—and far more challenging as well.

The reason is that virtually every aspect of business today is in the throes of change—and at a pace that is unprecedented in history. Familiar and well-documented factors—the emergence of a global economy, the remarkable advances in information technologies, the consolidation of many industries through multi-billion-dollar mergers, the changing demographics of the workplace—together have created competitive and operational pressures that most companies have never had to deal with before. With competition more intense than ever, companies can no longer afford the luxury of lengthy product development cycles, use price increases as a way to protect profit margins, or carry on their payrolls excessive numbers of employees who do not make a measurable contribution to the competitive effort.

It is no surprise, then, that everywhere in business today, whether it's a multinational company or a mom-and-pop retail operation we're talking about, there is a preoccupation with efficiency, cost control, responsiveness, and productivity. What clearly *doesn't* work today are the bureaucratic, multilayered management structures that were the defining characteristic of major corporations throughout the middle decades of the twentieth century. The inevitable push today, as we move toward the twenty-first century, is toward flatter, leaner structures with fewer controls, less supervision, and more autonomy for the people actually doing the work. And the inevitable result is that the performance bar for individual employees in virtually every industry has risen more appreciably over the past decade than in any other 10-year period in history. What most people do today at work—regardless of their responsibilities—is more technically complex, more varied, more customer-driven than it has ever been. To compound the challenge, the work is being conducted in an atmosphere that is far more pressured and far less predictable than before.

What does all of this mean for the hiring and staffing function in business today? Simply this: Traditional approaches to staffing and hiring no longer work for most companies in most industries; and companies that cling to these approaches do so at their own peril. In other words, it is no longer enough to bring to one's company or department employees who can merely meet the fundamental requirements of the position. The need today is for employees who can work productively in today's new, uncertain environment. As one might expect, the demand for such employees far outstrips the supply, which means, in turn, that unless a company has put into place a set of practices expressly designed to recruit, hire, and retain top performers, its ability to compete successfully in the coming decade will be severely compromised.

This chapter describes the key issues that underlie this new imperative and the impact these factors have on successful hiring and staffing strategies for the future.

THE TASK IS BOSS: REDEFINING THE BASIC CONCEPT OF "JOBS"

Until 15 to 20 years ago, most hiring decisions were driven by a common set of assumptions regarding the fundamental nature of jobs. It was generally assumed, for instance, that a company's operations could be broken down into a series of discrete positions—each position occupying its own place in the organizational chart, with its own set of reporting relationships, and entailing a specific range of responsibilities.

These assumptions are no longer as valid as they used to be. The multi-layered, top-town, rigidly hierarchical management structures of the past are slowly but surely disappearing from the corporate landscape. The accountabilities of the past are still in place, but, as everyone knows, the layers and layers of middle management that once separated senior management from front-line managers and employees have been significantly thinned and, in some companies, eliminated entirely.

Changing, too, is the nature of the boss/subordinate relationship. Increasingly in progressive companies, the true "boss" in any given situation isn't the man or woman who occupies the next rung on the corporate ladder. The *real* boss is the task at hand—the work that needs to be done. There is far more emphasis today in most companies on the broad mission—what the company must do as a whole to remain competitive—than there is on the individual tasks that people perform by way of carrying out that mission. *Who* does what and under whose command, in other words, becomes far less important than *what* gets done and how the customer is affected.

The traditional practice of organizing work according to specific jobs, each with its own job description, has given way to an elastic paradigm that can expand according to environment changes. Some have gone so far as to declare the "job," as we know it, is a thing of the past—a "dinosaur."[1]

That's probably an overstatement, but not by much. Employee empowerment, self-directed teams, increased reliance on contingent workers—these and other staffing initiatives that have come to the fore in recent years are all variations on the same theme. They reflect an effort to focus energy and resources more vigorously on what needs to be achieved to survive and compete successfully. This is the antithesis of getting bogged down with internal politics and turf issues.

At the core of this transformation is a concept we'll be looking at in more depth in the next chapter. It's called *strategic staffing,* an approach to staffing that is first and foremost geared to the needs of the business, both present and future.

Strategic staffing represents a major shift from the way the overall hiring function has traditionally been envisioned and managed. Its goal is to ensure that staffing decisions mirror what is actually going on in a company at any given time—ups and downs, seasonal fluctuations, business cycles, and more. In contrast to more traditional models of hiring, where strategies are often based on existing staffing structure, strategic staffing integrates hiring decisions into the overall business plan. Instead of "doing what you can with the people you have," with strategic staffing you first figure out what you need to do to compete effectively, and then determine how best to organize the internal and external human resources needed to meet your goal.

The approach isn't about "filling jobs." It's about mobilizing and managing the resources needed to get the job done, and also about making sure that all the various components of the hiring process—everything from how the basic job description is created to the way the interview and other assessment practices are handled—are driven by a consistent set of strategic priorities. Indeed, if there is any single theme that is sounded throughout all the chapters that follow, it is the notion of interdependence—that each step in the staffing process is guided to a great extent by some earlier strategic decision.

So when we get to Chapters 4, 5, and 6, which deal specifically with recruiting, screening, and interviewing, we will link the decisions that need to be made in each of these stages and decisions that were made earlier in the process.

It may surprise employers to learn that, according to a study by the Saratoga Institute, the average cost of hiring an external exempt worker is $8512.[2] This includes expenses for, among other things, advertising, staffing firms, travel, relocation, employee referral bonuses, and internal recruiting.

However, set aside these more obvious costs for a moment. While substantial, they do not take into account the hidden price of a careless hiring decision. Other factors to take into account include managerial time spent on recruiting and interviewing, as well as what did not get accomplished while managerial personnel focused on the hiring process.

Equally costly—and difficult to measure—is the disruption that occurs in a company when somebody new is hired, brought up to speed, and then let go, leaving a void that others in the company or department have to fill. Estimates vary, but some studies now show that whenever an employee fails to stay with a company for at least six months, the cost of replacing that person can be as much as two times the annual salary for his or her position.

On top of these expenses, businesses also must be aware of the legal ramifications—and potentially devastating costs—of termination-related lawsuits. Recent multi-million-dollar jury awards to individuals in such cases have made employers more vulnerable than ever to fallout from poor choices in personnel. At a minimum, regardless of the outcome of any such lawsuit, companies can incur significant legal expenses in defending legal actions by former staff members who were employed through faulty hiring practices.

KEY CONCEPT

THE IMPACT OF TECHNOLOGY

It is impossible to overstate the impact that technology has had—and will continue to have—on the industrialized world today. Few would deny that the most familiar trappings of modern-day technology—computers, copier machines, e-mail, voice mail, Internets and Intranets, and so on—have had a positive effect on productivity.

But there's a flip side to this. While technology has either streamlined or eliminated many of the routine and voluminous work functions, it has also created staffing challenges that many companies have yet to come to grips with. Companies that have invested heavily in technology usually find, for example, that they don't need as many employees on their payrolls as they once did. But they are also finding it increasingly difficult to recruit and retain so-called "knowledge workers"—workers with training to implement and maintain new technologies. Traditional job descriptions, as we will discuss in Chapter 3, no longer apply to most jobs that involve the use of technologically sophisticated equipment, and many of the hiring criteria that once prevailed in those jobs have become obsolete.

Another issue for a growing number of companies is whether the blinding pace of technological advancements is outstripping the ability to keep pace and utilize technology.

Frederick Reichhold, in *The Loyalty Effect,* maintains that the massive investments that many companies have made in automation throughout the late 1980s and early 1990s have failed in many cases to produce the bottom-line results that senior management had hoped to see.[3] The problem, in Reichhold's view, is not that the decision to invest in the technology was "wrong," but more that the companies failed to take into account and to effectively anticipate the collateral effects. There wasn't—and still isn't—enough attention given to the time, effort, and cost that need to be expended on training and on security measures. Noted management consultant Peter Drucker, among others, has begun to express concern that computers have dulled the strategic thinking of many senior managers. Computers, he says, tend to encourage "inward thinking": The process of actually using them can sometimes take precedence over the result they're designed to produce.[4]

The overall point here is not to disparage the importance of technology. It's to remind readers that technology, no matter how sophisticated it is, doesn't reduce the need for a well-thought-out, strategically driven approach to hiring. The need today, as we will be emphasizing throughout this book, is for balance: non-technically oriented employees who can be taught to tap the power of the new technologies, and technically oriented employees who can be taught to appreciate the basic dynamics of business.

THE CHANGING SOCIAL CONTRACT

A recently retired executive who had spent more than 30 years with the same company commented recently on how radically the culture had changed since he first joined the company in the mid-1960s.

When he first started with this company, the executive said, the message that came across to new hires was basically this: "Do your job well, fit in, keep your nose clean, and, one way or the other, you'll have a job for life." The message today, he maintains, goes more like this: "Here's an opportunity to perform. We'll give you the tools, we'll help you develop, and we'll reward you accordingly. That's all we can promise."

For better or worse, the message newly hired employees are now hearing from the managers in this particular company (either directly or implicitly) is the same message new hires are hearing today in most companies, large and small—and all the louder in companies that once prided themselves on their "cradle-to-grave" culture.

In light of the wrenching restructurings and layoffs that swept through most high-profile corporations during the 1980s and early 1990s, those on both sides of the hiring desk put much less stock in the concept of job security, especially those who were themselves casualties of downsizing. What's more, as Amanda Bennett points out in *Death of the Organization Man,* we will probably never return—certainly not in the foreseeable future—to the "one-company-for-life" mind-set that prevailed in many large companies throughout the middle decades of the twentieth century.[5] That mentality requires a business environment that is far more predictable and far less competitive than the one that exists today.

The underlying assumptions that govern the employer/employee relationship today have changed, and the implications cut both ways. Employees in general (Generation Xers, in particular) are resigned to the fact that in today's marketplace, corporate survival takes precedence over job security. Companies, however, are under more pressure than ever to make the work experience itself more interesting, more challenging, more rewarding.

The companies that are being penalized under this scenario, for now at least, are the major corporations, whose chief advantage over their smaller rivals has always been the fact that they could offer more job security, more perks, and more clearly defined (if slower) career paths than smaller companies could. "Most of my former students are bored working for large companies," Peter Drucker told *Forbes* magazine in a 1997 interview. "They switch to medium-size and small companies after a few years. The only reason they take jobs at large companies is they're the only ones recruiting on campus."[6]

The key lesson here: Corporations of all sizes and in every industry need to come to grips with the new quid pro quo. Today's top candidates no longer expect—or necessarily even want—cradle-to-grave security, and they are far too impatient to put any value on a gold watch at the end of a career. Still, they want something that has value beyond a regular paycheck. They want a job experience that has meaning, that will enable them to learn and grow, and that will move them down a career path that may (or may not) continue with their current company.

MANAGING DIVERSITY

Workplace diversity has been a front-burner issue in American business ever since the federal government, in the mid-1960s, enacted a sweeping set of initiatives and laws built around the principle of equal opportunity in the workplace. The difference today, however, is that diversity is no longer simply a legal or even a moral issue for people who hire. It has become a competitive, bottom-line issue as well. Companies with culturally and ethnically diverse workforces, for example, have often come to enjoy an edge in domestic and international markets. And even if this weren't the case, companies in highly competitive industries can ill afford, in today's tight labor market, to foster a culture that denies opportunity and discourages the contributions of the women and minorities who make up 64 percent of the American workforce. Farah M. Walters, president of University Health Systems, likens companies with progressive diversity practices to Ivy League colleges, whose ability to consistently attract the best students enables them to remain the best colleges. "Attracting the best," Walters says, "becomes a self-fulfilling prophecy that applies equally to the business world."[7]

The American workforce is far more demographically diverse today than it's ever been—and is destined to become even more diverse over the next decade. Statisticians may quibble about the rate of change and may have different ideas of what the changes mean, but the numbers speak for themselves. Women, according to 1995 census figures, currently account for 46 percent of the workforce, but have accounted for nearly 60 percent of the workforce growth between 1985 and 1995. At the same time, the proportion of minorities in the workforce (African Americans and Hispanics in particular) continues to rise and is projected to reach 20 percent by the year 2005.[8] The question is no longer whether companies need to factor diversity issues into all aspects of their hiring practices. That's a given. The real question is how they are going to manage this aspect of hiring in the most effective manner.

THE LIFESTYLE FACTOR

To an increasing number of American workers today, it takes more than an attractive salary and bonus package to make a job worth taking. More and more, there is growing interest as to the impact the job has on lifestyle and family life. This issue has profound implications for companies that are seeking to attract the top performers in the labor market.

The signs are everywhere. Job applicants, according to a Robert Half International survey conducted in 1996, are now twice as likely to ask questions about corporate culture during the job interview as they are to ask about job security. And, as *Forbes* magazine pointed out in a cover story in November 1996, progressive companies have begun to discover that while money is still the most important consideration for workers, nonmonetary, "lifestyle" perks have now become more important than before.[9]

The steps companies are taking to address the issue of lifestyle are many and varied, but they're all geared toward the same objective: to ease those non-work-related pressures that interfere with the ability of workers to do their best when they're on the job. Many companies today, for instance, have instituted flextime policies, giving employees the opportunities to create work schedules that make it easier to balance work responsibilities with family responsibilities. Others now include allowances for child care or elder care as part of their benefits packages.

"Employers with the best chances of attracting the best workers," according to *Forbes,* "are looking beyond money. They're looking at the psychological connections employees make with their employers and at whether they want their employees to work grudgingly as wage slaves, or energetically as committed members of a team."[10]

MORE READING

Bartlett, Christopher A. and Ghoshal, Sumantra. "Hanging the Role of Top Management: Beyond Systems to People." *Harvard Business Review* (May/June 1995).

Edmondson, Brad. "Workers With Attitude." *American Demographics* (April 1995).

Flynn, Gillian. "Xers vs. Teamwork." *Workforce* magazine, formerly known as *Personnel Journal* (November 1996).

Ramsey, Robert D. "Growth After Downsizing." *Supervision* (March 1997, vol. 58, no. 3), p. 5(4), Reference # A19363647.

Russell, Cheryl. "How Many Home Workers?" *American Demographics* (May 1996).

Seidler, Edward. "Discipline and Deselection in the TQM Environment." Total Quality Management Special Symposium—Adapting Assessment Systems to the TQM Environment. *Public Personnel Management* (Winter 1996).

Walters, Farah M. "Why the Right Thing to Do is Also the Smart Thing to Do." *Vital Speeches* (June 1, 1995).

CHAPTER 

Identifying Staffing Needs

INTRODUCTION

It is widely believed that the success or failure of any hiring decision depends mainly on what happens during the job interview—that is, how skillfully the interviewer is able to evaluate the candidate's qualifications and character on the basis of how the candidate performs during the interview. But seasoned hiring professionals know from direct experience that the ability to interview effectively represents only one aspect of a process consisting of many interrelated components that can go awry in any number of ways. They are also aware that most hiring "mistakes" do not result from erroneous judgments made during the job interview, but instead are rooted in missteps that occur much earlier in the process. No misstep carries a greater potential to sabotage the entire process than the failure to answer the most fundamental question of all: "What exactly do we need?"

This chapter looks closely at how the planning phase of the hiring process needs to be approached in light of the changing employment environment.

IT STARTS WITH WHAT THE JOB IS MEANT TO DO

Most of the articles and books written to date about the art of successful hiring have been built around a simple but dangerous assumption—that the job description, which usually serves as the basis for the entire hiring process—can be taken at face value and represents an accurate picture of what the organization actually needs.

This assumption can no longer be taken for granted. One way or the other, the hiring manager needs to take the time to make sure the job specifications, and the hiring criteria that emerge from those specifications, are logically keyed with the strategic needs of the business.

It wasn't always this way. In old-line, highly bureaucratic structures, job descriptions and the hiring criteria implicit in them were usually driven by the structure of the organization, not the strategic needs of the business. The typical job description was, in effect, an order that had to be filled. An opening would materialize. The job specifications tied to that opening would be retrieved (usually from a preexisting database). And the recruiting process would begin, with few people pausing long enough to say, "Wait, maybe those specifications are no longer as valid as they once were."

Fortunately, this pattern doesn't prevail as much as it used to. As organizational structures in companies have become flatter, the imaginary wall that used to separate the role of human resources managers in the hiring process from that played by line managers no longer exists. Human resources executives in progressive companies operate today under a new imperative: to work closely with front-line managers to bring staffing decisions in line with the company's mission, its values, and its strategic objectives.

It is not within the scope of this book to focus on how organizations develop mission statements, envision their futures, and set their strategic plans

Stellar Performer: University of Nebraska Medical Center

Symbolizing the New Partnership

The dynamics of the new, strategically driven approach to hiring can be seen in any number of organizations today but is well illustrated by the staffing process recently put into place at the University of Nebraska Medical Center. The Medical Center, like most organizations, had traditionally viewed its human resources department as a support function with no real strategic significance. Today, by contrast, it has a system whose primary purpose is to set into place a series of "integrated, organizationwide staffing strategies that anticipate and meet changing workforce requirements."[2]

The main difference between conditions then and now at the UNMC is that human resources personnel and unit managers today are working much more closely together in all phases of the staffing process. Unit managers are still responsible for putting together the strategic plan, but that plan is now a working document and not simply a blueprint that human resources personnel follow in their recruiting and hiring activities. Line managers and human resources specialists meet early in the process to review the staffing aspects of the plan, with much of the time devoted toward developing hiring criteria that reflect the "core behavioral and technical competencies" required to excel in each position. To complete the picture, staffing tasks that used to be handled independently—recruiting and compensation analysis, for instance—have been combined to better streamline the overall process, and there has been a concerted effort as well to develop and acquire technology that facilitates this streamlining.

The lesson to be drawn from what is happening at the University of Nebraska is not so much the specifics of the initiative, but the strategic intent behind it. The university symbolizes what is beginning to happen in large organizations throughout the world—that is, the collapse of the imaginary wall that has traditionally separated the activities of human resources specialists from the actual needs of line managers. Instead of performing their roles in isolation, these specialists now work together to meet the same basic challenge.

into place. Suffice it to say, however, that anyone involved in any way with hiring decisions needs to be tuned into the bigger picture. As Bob Bogart, executive vice president of human resources for Mutual of Omaha, puts it, "The very term 'personnel decision' has become an anachronism today. Everything has to be viewed within the context of the entire business."[1]

THE "REENGINEERING" FACTOR: MATCHING STRATEGIC GOALS TO CURRENT STAFFING REALITY

Chief among the differences between companies that are flourishing today and those that aren't is the flexibility of their staffing initiatives. The problem in many of the companies that are not competing effectively is not so much that they lack good products or innovative marketing initiatives; instead, the appropriate staffing infrastructures and philosophies capable of supporting these initiatives are not in place. Not enough thought is given in these companies to such fundamental questions as, "Do we have the people to carry out this initiative? Will we be able to give our people the training and the support they need to make the initiative a success?" Too many bold strategic initiatives fail in part because senior management has underestimated how difficult it is to get people to embrace change, even when change may be in everyone's best interest. Too often, senior management fails to generate the necessary resources and commitment to make the initiatives happen.

One company that didn't fall victim to this pitfall is the well-known Freeport, Maine-based retailer L.L. Bean.

L.L. Bean sells more than $1 billion worth of merchandise a year, virtually all through catalog and phone sales. The company sends out 130 million catalogs and handles more than 13 million catalog and service calls annually.

In contrast to many companies, L.L. Bean decided to make some fundamental changes in its staffing structure before it was under the gun to do so. "We felt that we couldn't rest on our past success at delighting our customers," explained Louis V. Zambello III, L.L. Bean's senior vice president of operations. "These days, the competition quickly duplicates what you do. It's a constant race to provide the best service."[3]

L.L. Bean began its reengineering initiative by carefully reviewing all its customer service operations, with an eye toward improving the quality of service provided. Whenever the company found what it perceived to be a "weakness"—a practice that a competitor might take advantage of—a strategic goal was set to overcome the weakness. When it was discovered, for instance, that a routine purchase or a simple return could sometimes take as long as two weeks to process, the company set a strategic goal of reducing that time frame in stages to under a week, then to four to five days, and finally to the current level—two days.

If L.L. Bean had simply announced these initiatives to its current staff, Zambello said, it's highly unlikely that the process would have worked. Zambello and others at the company were well aware, however, that the business process improvement efforts necessary to achieve these goals would mean some significant job content changes for the people involved. As he put it, "There weren't just winners. There were going to be some losers, too, in terms of losses in jobs or job status."

Zambello concedes that the process of getting employees to accept the new roles that were required by the new strategic initiatives didn't always go as smoothly as he would have liked. "A lot of people support the idea of reengineering," he said, "until it gets to the time where people see that some jobs are going to be lost and some job content is going to be changed, and somebody is going to have to sign on the bottom line for a process that nobody has really ever been through before." One of the problems at Bean, he reported, is that not everybody wanted to be accountable for the new goals.

Even so, the initiatives were eventually carried out successfully, and Zambello gave the credit to Bean's front-line leaders, who did not simply foist the new programs on the workforce, but went out of their way to provide the concrete measures that were required to make the effort a success. They communicated openly and frequently with employees; they created a genuine learning environment; they provided the incentives for people who were willing to go on the line for the initiatives; and, when necessary, they moved people who were not willing to support the program.

The ultimate staffing lesson, according to Zambello, was this: "What we found most important to eventual success was that the scope of the reengineering project must not creep up. If you're reengineering a service process to obtain growth, you may find everybody else in the company trying to get in at the same time— for instance, finance, to improve fraud detection capabilities; or human resources, to improve personnel tracking. If the scope creeps to encompass all these areas, we've found the project never gets done."

And how do you resist "scope creep"? In Zambello's view, you don't permit it to happen. "Somebody," he says, "needs to take responsibility for the process. Whoever that person is has to recognize he or she is not always going to be a very popular person, and to also recognize that it is better to have successfully implemented 60 percent of what your company wants than to have not quite implemented 100 percent of what your company wants. It's really a matter of discipline and being willing to make the hard, unpopular decisions. But as unpopular as you are during the process, once things are turned around you'll be very popular for getting something done." See Table 2.1 for a list of questions to ask yourself before beginning the hiring process.

HOW TO TELL WHEN STAFFING IS OUT OF SYNC WITH BUSINESS DEMANDS

DANGER!

The fact that a company is showing growth in both revenue and earnings doesn't necessarily mean that its staffing structure and policies are in productive sync with its operational and strategic needs. Often, in fact, a company is performing well in spite of its staffing policies and not because of them, and the danger here is twofold. For one

TABLE 2.1 SEVEN QUESTIONS THAT NEED TO BE ADDRESSED BEFORE THE HIRING PROCESS BEGINS

- What is the company's strategic vision?
- What are the company's long-term strategic goals?
- What are the company's goals in the near future?
- What changes, if any, are taking place in the marketplace that could have an impact on the company's future?
- What marketing or expansion initiatives are in place that would necessitate change in the company's hiring philosophy or practice?
- What changes in the structure of current jobs will be necessary to support the strategic vision?
- Who in the company is likely to resist the changes, and how will this resistance be overcome in a way that doesn't destroy morale?

thing, the current staffing problems could threaten the company's ability to sustain its growth; for another, should the business experience a downturn, the company may not have sufficient resources to respond. The critical symptoms typically found in a staffing structure that is out of sync with its business needs, even when the income statement is healthy, are as follows.

- *Frequent quality breakdowns:* events that could jeopardize customer relationships or put excessive pressure on employees. These include missed deadlines, an increase in products that need to be returned, work that needs to be redone, administrative mistakes, and so on. A good measurement: What percentage of time is now being spent on controlling the damage?
- *Excessive overtime:* a signal that current staff is becoming overburdened—which can lead to burnout. There is also the incremental cost to employees of overtime pay.
- *High turnover and absenteeism:* generally reliable signs that the workload and the staffing capacity are out of sync with each other. It could mean (1) that employees are looking for outside work; (2) that the stress of the work is taking its toll; or (3) poor morale.
- *Stressed-out employees:* usually observable as a general air of tension throughout the office or

factory, low energy, frequent bickering, employee complaints and negativity, and unusual sloppiness around work areas (a sign that employees don't care about appearances). Watch for grumbling on the employee grapevine—an indication that management is perceived as insensitive to employee needs.

Table 2.2 shows steps to take to harmonize hiring decisions with business objectives.

DON'T JUMP THE GUN

DANGER!

One of the hazards for companies beginning to think more strategically about their staffing needs might best be described as the "jumping the gun" pitfall. Example: A large customer service organization, in its rush to address what it believed to be weaknesses in its customer service department, launched a costly training and recruiting initiative in the mid-1990s that involved bringing in a highly trained staff of representatives capable of handling, with great efficiency, the most complex customer inquiries. Service improved, but the cost of maintaining the service was putting a strain on the company's resources. The company analyzed its operations and found that 80 percent of the customer inquiries involved

TABLE 2.2 A FOUR-STEP PROCESS FOR BRINGING HIRING DECISIONS INTO ALIGNMENT WITH STRATEGIC OBJECTIVES

- Look at overall objectives of the company's business plan and take note of the key objectives (i.e., saving money, increasing profitability, expanding geographically, and so on).
- Assess and analyze the skills workers currently have and compare these with the specific skills and capabilities needed to successfully accomplish the objectives.
- Differentiate between skills that are critical to core competencies, as opposed to those that could conceivably be provided by supplemental staffing (e.g., administrative, manufacturing, or professional employees brought in on a temporary basis).
- Get a clear fix on the gaps that exist between future needs and current capabilities and begin to formulate a plan designed to eliminate the gap.

only 8 to 10 questions, which meant that the company was now overstaffed with high-level specialists who were answering basic, routine questions—a classic case of inefficient staff deployment. Had the company done some careful analysis, it could have put together a much less costly operation, one that would have required fewer highly trained employees (see Table 2.3).

KEY CONCEPT

CREATING THE JOB DESCRIPTION

Depending on how the process of creating and writing it is handled, a job description can be either a straitjacket that limits the ability of an individual or group to make creative and resourceful decisions, or a tool that enhances everyone's ability to think "outside the box."

TABLE 2.3 KEY QUESTIONS TO THINK ABOUT DURING THE PLANNING PROCESS

- Why has the need for this job arisen? Is it in response to new business demand or to an operational problem that might lend itself to a solution other than hiring somebody new?
- Who (if anybody) is currently performing these tasks, how long have they been performing these tasks, how well are they performing the tasks, and what role (if any) should these people play in the selection of an employee to perform similar tasks?
- What will be the initial goals of this position and how long will it take to accomplish them?
- Is there enough work to warrant a full-time position? Or might there be some other way of handling the task? Perhaps a part-timer, supplemented by temporaries or consultants during peak periods, could suffice.
- Can some of the overload duties be switched to another area within the same department or location?
- Is this a true need or can the systems in this function be streamlined for better productivity?
- How much will this new position cost?
- Is there a sufficient supply of qualified job candidates from which to choose?
- Have all the parties who will be affected by this new hire been informed of the situation and is there a consensus regarding the need?
- How long will it take for the new hire to get up to speed?
- What impact will the creation of this new position have on the jobs from which the tasks are being removed?
- What is the worst that can happen if this position is not created?[4]

Everybody agrees that *some* form of documentation needs to serve as the basis of the hiring process. The current debate has to do with what form the job description ought to take and how the process of getting it down on paper should be organized and carried out. A growing number of companies today—British Petroleum, for instance—have virtually abandoned the traditional approach to job descriptions (i.e., individual job specifications that characterize specific jobs in the organizational chart). They have replaced it with a much more fluid, matrixlike approach. The job description is focused on the general tasks that need to be performed on a departmentwide and companywide basis and includes the competencies required to perform those tasks.[5] The service department of the company, for instance, will take a close look at its current practices to determine what needs to be done to meet customer needs. It will base its hiring strategies on those requirements rather than the specific tasks that might be associated with an individual position. The position may still exist, but the hiring criteria will usually be broader and more customer-directed.

The following are some general principles regarding the preparation of job descriptions that reflect this progressive new model.

Don't take anything for granted. Each new hiring situation should propel everyone involved in the hiring process to reevaluate the relevance of the existing job description. Written job descriptions have a tendency to change over time, not according to the needs of the business but according to the strengths, weaknesses, likes, and dislikes of the person who filled the job. In fact, many hiring consultants advise their clients to take with a grain of salt any feedback that originates from the person who previously held the job. It isn't that the former jobholders deliberately lie. It's more the natural tendency of people to exaggerate the difficulty of those aspects of the job they didn't handle particularly well.

Consult others. As organizations become flatter and more collaborative, it becomes increasingly important for job descriptions to be envisioned and analyzed with an eye toward group dynamics. This phenomenon applies in particular to companies committed to an entrepreneurial culture in which front-line employees make decisions that formerly originated several levels higher. It is also critical, obviously, for companies that are committed to the concept known as self-directed teams. In more and more team-based companies—Saturn, for instance—hiring issues that affect the makeup of a team are invariably addressed by that team, which is often empowered to establish its own job specifications, develop its own parameters for hiring, and, in some instances, determine compensation and bonus packages.

Be realistic. It is one thing to put together an elaborate description of what tasks a job will most likely entail, and another to identify what skills and traits are needed to perform that job well. But, quite apart from being aligned with business needs, job descriptions need to define a job that is fillable given current market conditions and what the company is prepared to pay. A useful reality check is to take each of the tasks that are required and create a rough estimate of how long it would take a person with average skills to perform each of those tasks in a typical day or week. Whenever the weekly hours begin to dramatically exceed 40, there's a good chance that the job description is far too ambitious and not likely to lead to a satisfying result.

Table 2.4 shows the benefits resulting from use of a good job description.

TABLE 2.4 WHAT A WELL-EXECUTED JOB DESCRIPTION CAN ACCOMPLISH

- Establishes the framework for analyzing appropriate hiring criteria
- Gives candidates a clear idea of what to expect and helps to weed out candidates who are clearly unsuited for the job
- Helps determine the pay range of the job, based on market value for the various tasks that are performed
- Works as a tool for setting expectations and setting up objective measures for performance appraisal
- Provides a preliminary idea of how easy or difficult it will be to find someone to fill the job

Make sure the wording of a job description is in compliance with Equal Employment Opportunity Commission (EEOC) regulations. There should be no mention of age, gender, marital status, religion, or ethnic background.

JOB DESCRIPTIONS AND EMPLOYEE RETENTION

A study conducted in the early 1990s found that an effectively written job description could have a significant impact on employee turnover in the insurance industry.[6] The retention rates were compared between two groups of agents: those who had been given an "accurate and sufficient description" of the job they were about to take and those who weren't. The results: Agents who had been given an accurate and sufficient description were twice as likely to be on the job two years later than agents who weren't. The retention rate was even more striking when the limit was stretched to three years.

MAKE THE JOB DESCRIPTION REAL-WORLD

Before any hiring criteria can be established, the information on the basic job description form needs to be fine-tuned in two key areas: The information that appears under the "principal tasks" category needs to be prioritized, and the hiring criteria need to be checked and double-checked to make sure that they are an accurate reflection of what it takes to succeed in the job. See Table 2.5 for a basic job description outline.

Prioritizing Principal Tasks

Any familiar system of prioritization can work (1–5 or A,B,C) when determining which tasks in any given job description are the most important; the idea is to gain some perspective into the relative importance of each task based on current conditions in the company.

Hiring Criteria

If the process to this point has been strategically driven, it should now be possible to develop some

TABLE 2.5 A JOB DESCRIPTION OUTLINE

The following categories represent a rough template of what a typical job description might look like and what specific information it should convey.

Job title (if applicable).

General description. Two or three sentences to sum up the overall responsibilities of the person who performs this job.

Reports to. The person in the company who will supervise or manage the person who eventually fills this job.

Principal tasks. The specific tasks that the person or people who will be doing this job will be asked to carry out on a day-to-day basis.

Basic hiring requirements. Anything in the way of licensing, certification, or training that a person hired *must* have in order to be eligible for the job.

Hiring criteria. The criteria that will be used to evaluate candidates (i.e., the skills, background, knowledge, or traits required to perform the job well).

hiring criteria for each of the tasks, with emphasis on those tasks that have the highest priorities. Here are three key ideas to bear in mind.

1. *Make a distinction between required credentials, skills, and traits.*
   - *Credentials:* anything in the way of licensing or certification without which the person would not be permitted to handle the job. Tip: Make sure they are logically tied to the requirements of the job.
   - *Skills:* which competencies the candidate must possess to handle the job well. (Don't worry for now about how easy or difficult it might be to train someone.)
   - *Traits:* these apply not only to the job at hand but to other aspects of the work experience, such as the personality and working style of the supervisor, the general environment or culture in the company, and so forth.
2. *Make the criteria as specific and as detailed as possible:* The more comprehensive and specific the hiring criteria are, the easier it will be to organize all the other aspects of the hiring process.

SAMPLE JOB DESCRIPTIONS

Job Title: Controller.

General Description:

Directs the general accounting function. Has overall responsibility for the following areas: financial reporting, corporate tax, budgeting, stock administration, bonus, staff payroll, payroll tax, general ledger, accounts payable, cash management, and insurance.

Reports to: Chief financial officer.

Principal Tasks:

- Manages all aspects of SEC reporting.
- Coordinates auditor, legal, and management review of all financial transactions.
- Manages complex technical issues and special projects.
- Prepares a monthly reporting package for internal management and a quarterly reporting package for the CFO, including detailed analysis of P&L trends, balance sheet trends, and cash flow.
- Responsible for corporate taxes, including federal, state, property, and sales tax returns and compliance audits.
- Manages the following: filings of all federal, state, and local payroll tax returns; all bank accounts; payment processing of monthly invoices; annual budget process; insurance contracts; debt compliance and cash.
- Manages a staff of approximately 40 individuals.

Basic Hiring Requirements:

CPA license and a bachelor's degree in accounting or finance.

Hiring Criteria:

- Minimum of eight years of financial and accounting experience, with at least three years of SEC reporting experience in a public accounting firm or in the financial reporting department of a public corporation.
- Proven management and problem-solving skills and ability to motivate employees.
- Excellent computer skills, including proficiency in the use of spreadsheet programs, and the ability to quickly acclimate to complex financial accounting applications.
- Excellent organizational, written, and verbal communications skills.
- The ability to work long hours during peak workloads such as year- and quarter-end, and during special projects.

Job Title: Administrative assistant.

General Description:

Provides administrative support to the marketing manager.

Reports to: Marketing manager.

(Continued)

(Continued)

Principal Tasks:

- Maintains manager's schedule and coordinates travel arrangements.
- Sorts and prioritizes mail.
- Prepares correspondence.
- Maintains filing systems.
- Prepares presentations and reports.
- Completes special projects as required.

Basic Hiring Requirements:

Associate's degree in business or equivalent combination of education and experience. Excellent communications and word processing skills.

Hiring Criteria:

Prior experience in similar industry and proficiency in presentation software highly desirable. Ability to work as part of a team with administrative assistants in other departments.

Job Title: Product marketing manager.

General Description:

Responsible for the success of a specific product line in the U.S. market through execution of a comprehensive marketing plan.

Reports to: Division manager.

Principal Tasks:

- Develops and implements a marketing program for a specific product line.
- Conceptualizes and implements product launches for the U.S. market.
- Works with sales and manufacturing areas to strategize product development and positioning, and monitors customer responses and market trends to help facilitate this.
- Prepares pricing proposals for new and existing products, and manages complete product life cycle.
- Coordinates customer training.

Basic Hiring Requirements:

Bachelor's degree and five years of marketing experience. Excellent communications skills a must.

Hiring Criteria:

MBA with one year of industry experience.

3. *Give the process time:* The more time taken in the beginning to develop a full and accurate job description, the more likely the process will produce results. Resist the temptation to simply "find a body," even when there's intense pressure to fill the job quickly. The cost and the disruption of a hiring "mistake" far outweigh whatever time and effort are necessary to create a strong job description.

Once the job description has been created (manually or with the use of software—see Table 2.6)—the next step is to develop an appropriate salary range. There are several resources available, including classified ads, professional and trade associations (many conduct salary surveys), human resources consultants, recruiters that specialize in

TABLE 2.6 PUTTING SOFTWARE TO WORK

Companies looking for software packages that bring added efficiency and precision to the job description process have more choices today than ever before, but the programs have limitations and need to be chosen with care. The principal minus is that the job descriptions generated by these programs are, by nature, highly general: They use job categories, tasks, and other data that are more geared to traditional environments than to today's workplace. Companies contemplating the purchase of these programs should recognize that they work well as a tool in the process but can't be expected to provide genuine strategic guidance. Companies should never assume, either, that the descriptions generated by these programs fall within EEOC guidelines.

The following are factors to consider when purchasing software.

- Is it compatible with the company's existing computer hardware and software?
- Does the software company offer upgrades designed to keep pace with changes in EEOC regulations and labor laws? If so, is there a charge?
- Do the job classifications that exist on the software match the jobs that exist within the company?
- Is the program user-friendly? (How good are the documentation and assorted tutorials?)
- Can it be edited or adapted to a company's own database?
- How flexible are its search options?

the fields for which you are hiring, and career centers. The U.S. Bureau of Labor Statistics publishes the *Occupational Outlook Handbook* containing job descriptions and salaries for virtually every field.

When establishing a salary range, specific requirements of the job, such as unusual hours, necessary credentials, years of experience, and specialized training, should be taken into consideration. Other factors to take into account include the company's growth rate and geographic location; the cost of living; and availability of qualified candidates.

For example, if you are planning to hire a candidate, you can access the aforementioned sources to determine a salary range appropriate to the size of your company. Because it is likely that you will end up with an average range for the nation, you can then add or subtract from the amount depending on the cost of living in your area and other unique factors.

When it comes to establishing a salary range, keep in mind that paying a little more than your competition may help ensure that you attract and retain outstanding individuals. In addition to salary, consider alternate forms of compensation such as 401(k) and pension plans, stock options, and profit sharing.

HOW BENCHMARKING TOP PERFORMERS CAN PRODUCE VALID HIRING CRITERIA

One of the most significant trends in hiring today is the practice of benchmarking top performers in a particular function to develop a targeted, reliable hiring criteria. In some instances, benchmarking is conducted on an informal basis—the company owner or its senior managers may simply have conversations with those employees who excel at a particular set of tasks. In other instances, the process is much more structured, often involving outside consultants and extensive testing. In either case, the goal is the same: to identify a common set of competencies that characterize the top performers in any specific area of the business, and, on the basis of those competencies, create an "ideal candidate profile."

Typical of companies that have adopted this approach is Doubletree Corporation, the Phoenix-based hotel firm, whose vice president of human resources, Ann Rhoades, was formerly with Southwest Airlines. Described recently by the magazine *Fast Company* as "something of a legend in hiring circles," Rhoades is a disciple of the hiring methodology generally known as targeted selection.[7] Targeted selection is built around the premise that the best way to select new employees is to first identify the key behaviors and attitudes of people who are already performing at high levels in the company, and then develop a set of interview questions designed to find people with those attributes. Working with Development Dimensions International, a Pittsburgh-based consulting company, Rhoades engineered such a process for reservation clerks and identified "eight dimensions of success on the job": (1) practical learning; (2) teamwork; (3) adaptability; (4) tolerance for stress; (5) sales ability; (6) attention to detail; (7) flexibility; and (8) motivation.

What is particularly noteworthy about these attributes is that each has a specific behavioral counterpart that is intrinsically linked to the demands of the job. The behavioral component for flexibility, for example, is the ability to handle each call on an individual basis. To round out the process, Rhoades and her staff have developed a set of exercises that give interviewers a way of judging the extent to which candidates exemplify these competencies.

Variations of the benchmarking technique are taking place in thousands of companies worldwide, albeit with mixed results. The differentiator, not surprisingly, is how diligently the process is being carried out. "The main thing that people have to bear in mind when they go through this benchmarking process is that it needs to be done in depth," says Robert Fuller, an HR specialist with Siemens Medical Systems, who spent more than a year developing a set of core competencies for the company's sales force. Fuller warns that it isn't enough to simply pick out a couple of top performers, find out what they do, and then use that data as the basis of hiring criteria. "You need a reasonably large sampling, and you need to take into account the marketplace and the company culture. And you have to be careful that what people are telling you is valid. What we found when we began interviewing top performers is that a great many of them, good as they were, had difficulty articulating what made them so successful. In any event, off-the-shelf approaches don't work."[8]

Tip

DRAWING BEHAVIORAL CONNECTIONS

If benchmarking is to be used as a tool for establishing hiring criteria, it must allow interviewers to confirm desired on-the-job behaviors through some means of tangible observation or measurement. For example, among the 17 core competencies used by Cheetah Communications in Irvine, California, is something the company president, Dave Wiegand, calls "healthy self-talk." This, according to Wiegand, is the internal dialogue that highly successful salespeople go through when they're running into rejection after rejection. He has found that top performers in sales, as a rule, tend to be their own cheerleaders: When the going gets tough, they're able to buck themselves up. The specific behavioral mechanism Wiegand uses to uncover that trait is to ask candidates for sales positions what they would say to another salesperson who was running into rejections or having difficulty making appointments. "The answer you get in that situation," says Wiegand, "is usually what the salesperson would say to himself."[9]

JOB DESCRIPTIONS AND THE AMERICANS WITH DISABILITIES ACT

DANGER!

The passage of the Americans with Disabilities Act (ADA), which went into effect in January 1992, has helped to broaden the scope of job opportunities for people with disabilities. At the same time, it has complicated the process of formulating job descriptions that do not violate the intent and spirit of the law. The key point: Employers must be able to prove that the requirements listed in the job descriptions are authentically job related and do not create barriers to people with disabilities. Employers need to be aware, too, that they are now under obligation to make certain general accommodations in their workplace design and practices to meet the special needs of disabled individuals.

FACTORING IN THE COMPANY CULTURE

Every company, regardless of its size or industry, has a culture or environment and a set of values that have a significant impact on how people handle their jobs and interact with one another. Culture determines the unwritten rules of day-to-day business life: how early people come to work and how late they stay; how much autonomy people have; how they communicate (face-to-face, or by memo or e-mail); how much interaction there is between senior management and the front line; and how "casual" the rules are (if there are rules).

The issue here isn't whether one culture is superior to another but whether the staffing policies are consistent with whatever environment prevails. Here are some of the key factors relating to corporate culture that should be taken into consideration when job descriptions are being developed.

- *Performance standards and competitive environment:* How high are the performance standards in the company, and how do those standards figure into the company's overall mission and long-term goals? Does the company go out of its way to reward top performers?
- *Learning curve:* Does the company typically take the time to train and develop new candidates, or are new hires expected to "hit the ground running?"
- *Work ethic:* What is a "normal" workday in the company? Is it typically 9 to 5, five days a week

(very rare today in most companies); or do people routinely come early, stay late, and frequently work on weekends?

- *Management style:* Does the prevailing supervisory style in the company follow the traditional model (one manager or supervisor closely monitoring the work of direct reports), or are people largely expected to manage themselves?
- *Sense of family:* What importance (if any) does the company attach to "fitting in" to the corporate "family"? Is the company a place that encourages conformity or fosters individuality?

END POINT

The process progressive companies are now using to establish hiring criteria differs considerably from traditional approaches, and this difference starts with the way job descriptions are being written and used. The "cookie-cutter" approach is slowly but surely being abandoned for a much more integrated approach to establishing hiring criteria that takes into account the overall needs of the business. Companies have begun to rethink their own hiring criteria in an effort to establish guidelines that represent the true barometers of successful performance. One approach gaining popularity is identifying top performers in an organization, determining which specific skills and traits they embody, and then building job specifications and hiring criteria around those "core competencies."

For this undertaking to work, however, companies must be willing to devote sufficient time and effort to the process, and they need to factor the company's culture into the process.

MORE READING

Bechet, Thomas P. and James W. Walker, "Aligning Staffing With Business Strategy." *Human Resource Planning* (June 1993, vol. 16, no. 2), p. 1(16).

Bergin, Sarah. "Flexible Employees: Your Most Valuable Resources." *Transportation & Distribution* (March 1996, vol. 37, no. 3), p. 112(3), Reference # A18160864.

Braus, Patricia. "Sorry, Boys—Donna Reed is Still Dead." *American Demographics* (September 1995).

Burdman, Pamela. "Flexible Jobs on the Rise." *San Francisco Chronicle* (August 1992).

Denka, Andrew. "Achieve Better Management Through Strategic Staffing (Strategic Staffing Brings Just-In-Time Practices to the Office)." *Managing Office Technology* (March 1994, vol. 39, no. 3), p. 10(5).

Dobrynski, Judith. "Somber News for Women on the Corporate Ladder." *The New York Times* (November 6, 1996).

Forst, Leland I. "Fulfilling the Strategic Promise of Shared Services." *Strategy & Leadership* (Jan/Feb 1997, vol. 25, no. 1), p. 30(5).

Galagan, Patricia A. "Strategic Planning Is Back." *Training & Development* (April 1997).

Hamel, Gary and C K. Prahalad, "Strategic Intent." *Harvard Business Review* (May/June 1989).

Kennedy, Marilyn Moats. "A Nightmare Scenario: Managing Permanent and Part-time Employees." in "Up the Organization" column. *Across the Board* (July/August 1993, vol. 30, no. 6), p. 11(2).

Laabs, Jennifer J. "Why HR Is Turning to Outsourcing." *Workforce* magazine, formerly known as *Personnel Journal* (September 1993, vol. 72, no. 9), pp. 92–101.

Messmer, Max. "Achieving Quality Improvement Through Strategic Staffing." *Business Credit* (September 1993).

Shareef, Reginald. "A Popperian View of Change in Innovative Organizations." *Human Relations* (June 1997, vol. 50, no. 6), p. 655(16), Reference # A19621767.

Sunoo, Brenda Paik and Patricia L. Williams, "From Santa to CEO—Temps Play All Roles." *Workforce* magazine, formerly known as *Personnel Journal* (April 1996, vol. 75, no. 4), pp. 34–44.

Townsend, Bickley. "Room at the Top for Women." *American Demographics* (July 1996).

Wiley, Carolyn. "A Comparison of Seven National Temporary and Staffing Agencies." *Employment Relations Today* (Summer 1995, vol. 22, no. 2), p. 69(23).

Zinno, Vincent. "Beyond Strategic Staffing." *Human Resource Executive* (October 1996).

CHAPTER 

Strategic Staffing: The New Paradigm of Hiring

INTRODUCTION

The basic goal of hiring is the same today as it's always been. One way or another, businesses and other organizations need to find an efficient and cost-effective way to attract, hire, and retain quality employees—people who can help a company achieve its strategic goals. What's changing, however, is the mind-set that is now driving the hiring process, as well as the strategies that companies are adopting to fill their staffing needs. Savvy managers and business owners now recognize that the traditional model of hiring—finding individuals who meet the requirements of a "position"—is out of step with the challenges of today's business environment. It's too inflexible. It severely limits a company's ability to respond effectively to the changing dynamics of both the marketplace and the workplace. The need today is for staffing strategies that are fluid and flexible.

The new thinking that underlies the staffing practices of enlightened companies today is commonly referred to as *strategic staffing, flexible staffing, rightsizing,* or *optimal staffing*. Whatever the designation, the core idea is the same: to bring staffing policies and decisions into closer alignment with the direct needs of the business *as those needs arise*. The basic idea, in other words, is not to "fill desks" but to "fill needs." The old hiring approach was driven by the question, "What individual is best qualified to fill this position?" The new paradigm is driven by the question, "What combination of resources will best enable us to meet our short-term and long-term business needs?"

This chapter reviews the main options available to companies that are looking at new and creative ways to meet their staffing needs, and addresses the growing use of temporary workers as a fundamental staffing strategy.

KEY CONCEPT

A PROCESS, NOT A FORMULA

The term *strategic staffing* does not refer to one specific staffing option or technique. It refers instead to a mind-set—an overall approach to hiring and staffing that takes any number of forms (see Table 3.1). Here are three examples of how the concept is manifesting itself in a variety of organizations throughout America.

1. The California-based aerospace giant McDonnell Douglas is one of a rapidly growing number of government contractors that has incorporated into its operating plan a staffing strategy that combines a core group of full-time

TABLE 3.1 STRATEGIC STAFFING DEFINED

Staffing decisions can be defined as truly strategic if, apart from the impact they have on head count and dollars, they meet all of the following criteria.

- They are directly tied to the strategic goals of the business, both short- and long-term.
- They are consistent with a company's mission and its values.
- They strengthen a company's ability to focus the bulk of its energies on its core competencies—the qualities that differentiate it from the competition.

workers supplemented (on an as-needed basis) with a temporary or contingent workforce. The company's decision to move in this direction was driven in part by the desire to control overhead costs by converting fixed expenses to variable expenses. Just as important, though, was the determination to break free of the crippling and demoralizing cycles of large-scale hirings followed by layoffs or workweek reductions that are all too common in companies that rely on government contracts for a major part of their business.[1]

2. A small but growing number of major corporations—AT&T and 3M, to name just two—have organized their own internal contingency work forces. These internal pools are made up of full-time employees whose jobs have been eliminated but who remain as salaried employees for an extended period, working for various departments on an as-needed or project basis. These individuals are given the first opportunity to be considered for any openings that materialize in the company.[2]

3. One of the ways Aligned Fiber Composites (AFC), a manufacturing firm based in Chatfield, Michigan, has been able to reduce the costs of recruitment and turnover is to make temporary assignments a fixed part of its prescreening process. Instead of recruiting and hiring employees in the traditional manner, AFC hires prospects on a 90-day temporary basis, using outside temporary staffing services to handle recruitment and initial testing.

Their differences apart, each of these examples is rooted in the same general principle and objective: to fill a staffing need in a manner other than the traditional one-person, one-job model. These situations are not simply isolated examples of a trend destined to run out of steam in a few years. On the contrary, they exemplify what nearly all agree will be the norm in the years to come. It is generally agreed by most observers that by the twenty-first century, perhaps as many as 50 million positions will be outside of the 9-to-5, 40-hour week tradition.[3]

IT'S NOT SIMPLY ABOUT "HEAD COUNT"—OR DOLLARS

DANGER!

More often than not, strategic staffing practices enable companies to operate with fewer full-time employees and a greater contingent workforce. When implemented intelligently, these policies help companies control their overhead costs and operate more efficiently in general. But companies that base their alternate staffing strategies solely on these two concerns—head count and dollars—are missing the point and are almost certain to pay a stiff price for their shortsightedness. A study conducted by the American Management Association in 1995 found that fewer than half the firms that had undergone major downsizings in the five previous years were reporting higher profits and that only one-third were realizing higher productivity.[4]

As Frederick Reichheld points out in *The Loyalty Effect,* the typical pattern of public companies that undergo massive downsizings in order to shore up their stock prices is to show a slight gain during the first six months following the downsizings, followed by a sharp, steady lag. "This should really come as no surprise," Reichheld observes. "Companies forced to jettison human assets should be worth less—in the same way that a ship that jettisons part of its cargo will be worth less when it finally arrives in port."[5]

Savvy Wall Street investors no longer see large-scale downsizing as a positive sign. On the contrary, large-scale downsizings are now seen as a reliable indicator that management is not thinking strategically. Granted, in periods of crisis, a company has little choice but to operate as close to the bone as possible, but the ultimate goal of any staffing strategy is not simply to streamline but to strengthen a company's ability to serve the needs of its customers.

As Michael Hammer points out in *Reengineering the Corporation: A Manifesto for Business Revolution,* downsizing for the sake of downsizing is a generally ineffective response to a business crisis. In Hammer's view, these cutbacks only make sense under two conditions: (1) when there are gross amounts of fat in a company's organizational structure; and (2) when the company is contemplating a long-term decline in the demand for its products or services.[6]

One of the enduring lessons of the Malcolm Baldrige National Quality Award competition is that the journey to quality requires workers who are not only efficient and productive but highly motivated as well. Staffing strategies that do not produce this result are doomed to fail, regardless of how many heads roll and how much money is saved in the short term.

SELLING ALTERNATE STAFFING STRATEGIES—TO STAFF

It is wrong to assume that full-time employees will automatically view alternate staffing strategies as a threat to their job security and thus go out of their way to prevent company initiatives in this direction. The truth is that most people in the workforce today are far more receptive to new ideas than many senior managers realize. The chronic complaint heard throughout business today is not simply that employees are working too hard, but that too often they are working hard at tasks that are really peripheral to their core assignments and to the business as a whole.

TEMPORARY EMPLOYEES AS AN OVERALL STAFFING STRATEGY

Probably the most significant trend in strategic staffing today is the increasingly pivotal role that temporary workers are now assuming in the overall staffing mix of companies in virtually every industry (see Table 3.2). The use of temporary workers in and of itself is hardly a new phenomenon. Temporary staffing services have been around for more than 50 years, and companies large and small have routinely relied on temporary employees to either supplement the efforts of full-time workers at different times of the year or fill in

TABLE 3.2 WHY TEMPORARY STAFFING HAS GAINED FAVOR

The dramatic growth in the use of temporary and contract workers during the 1990s can be attributed to the following general factors.

- An increasing number of managers and business owners who see temporary staffing as a means of increasing flexibility and responsiveness to changes in business.
- An increase in the number of professionals who see long-term temporary and contract assignments as a viable alternative to traditional full-time jobs.
- The growing number of job seekers using temporary work as a means to explore different work environments before committing to full-time positions.
- A widespread reluctance among large companies that underwent massive downsizings during the 1980s to repeat the overstaffing practices that set the stage for downsizings.
- The tightening labor supply in certain key fields, which has severely limited the ability of many companies to access badly needed skills and meet certain critical staffing requirements with full-time personnel.
- A growing willingness on the part of companies both large and small to create work arrangements that make it easier for temporary employees to make meaningful contributions.
- The benefit to employers of "temp-to-hire" practices—using temporary assignments as a means of evaluating candidates for full-time positions.

when full-time employees are ill, on vacation, or on maternity leave.

The difference today is twofold.

To begin with, the number of temporary employees in the American workforce on any given day has grown dramatically. Companies recognize that by bringing in temporaries for peak periods, they can avoid overstaffing—specifically the hire/fire syndrome—and thus better protect the jobs of their long-term core employees.

The second big difference has to do with the changing nature of temporary work. It used to be that the vast majority of temporary assignments involved clerical or administrative tasks. And it was safe to assume that whenever someone who was well educated was working as a temporary, he or she viewed the process as merely a stopgap measure, not one that would necessarily lead to a full-time job.

Neither of these assumptions is valid today. True, the majority of temporary assignments still involve clerical and administrative work, and the majority of people working on temporary assignments (78 percent, according to the National Association of Temporary and Staffing Services)[7] are looking for full-time positions.

But the scenario on the whole is changing—and in a multitude of ways (see Table 3.3). Anywhere from 15 to 20 percent of the people working on a temporary assignment on any given day are college graduates (8 percent have advanced degrees), and a growing proportion are professionals—lawyers, teachers, architects, accountants, engineers, and computer programmers who may not necessarily be interested in finding full-time positions.[8] This ranges from professionals who want to devote more time to their families and/or personal pursuits to those in semiretirement.

The motivations, however, are pretty much the same. Many professionals on the temporary career track like what they do: Higher-level temporary positions or contract consulting in particular often provide the variety, challenge, and flexibility that a full-time position cannot.

This is all good news for companies that need the special expertise that professionals and spe-

TABLE 3.3 THE TEMPORARY WORKFORCE AT A GLANCE

Here's a statistical look at the fastest-growing segment of the American workforce, according to the National Association of Temporary and Staffing Services (NATSS).

Average daily number of people in the workforce working temporary assignments in 1982: 406,700

In 1990: 1,165,200

In 1996: 2,310,800

Temporary help payroll increased from $547 million in 1970 to $31.5 billion in 1996.

Percentage of temporary assignments that become full-time jobs: 30

Percentage of temporary professionals as part of the overall temporary workforce: 25

cialists can offer, but do not have the internal structure or the resources to hire these professionals on a full-time basis. These trends have also helped to fuel the growth of temporary staffing firms. Yearly revenues in the temporary services industry are expected to exceed $54 billion in 1997, and the fastest-growing segment of that industry is made up of companies who specialize in placing accountants, computer specialists, lawyers, teachers, scientists, and other professionals.[9] Overall payroll for temporary professionals is rising five times faster than the increase in payroll for all other temporaries in general.[10]

One of the most interesting by-products of this ongoing trend is the general change in the way in which temporary work is now perceived. When executives were asked in a 1994 Accountemps survey whether they considered a long period of consistent temporary work listed on a resume comparable to full-time employment, 78 percent answered "yes."

KEY CONCEPT

FLEXIBILITY IS KEY

Companies today call on temporary services for a variety of reasons, but the number one reason by far is to give the company greater staffing flexibility to meet unexpected workloads. In the past, business downturns often left companies with the choice of two negative outcomes: (1) retaining full-time personnel even though there wasn't enough work for them to do or (2) instituting mass layoffs or reduced workweeks.

In a 1996 Accountemps survey, 91 percent of executives surveyed from 150 of the nation's 1000 largest companies stated they were staffing more strategically than before. This included taking a long-term, big-picture view of staffing needs, and taking into account seasonal and other fluctuations. Businesses are becoming more aware of the cost and trauma associated with massive fluctuations in staffing levels.

A classic example of this staffing syndrome existed at Revcor, Inc., a Carpentersville, Illinois-based company that manufactures fans, wheels, and housings for air conditioning and heating components. As is typical of many manufacturing companies, the workload at Revcor was much more intense during certain times than at others. And traditionally, according to its human resources director, Larry Brigman, the company operated in a "lay off when we're slow, re-hire when we're busy syndrome." That approach, says Brigman, eventually caught up with the company, as Revcor became known as a company "you couldn't stay with."

Brigman's solution was to analyze the ebbs and flows of manufacturing on a yearly basis, and then devise a flexible staffing strategy that took those ebbs and flows into account. The result was a staffing strategy that combined a core group of 300 employees, who would then be supplemented by as many as 100 temporary workers during the busy season. This basic change in hiring strategy enabled the company to offer full-time workers far more assurance than had previously been the case, and, by doing so, brought to the company full-time employees who were qualified and motivated.[11]

A different situation involves Micros Systems, Inc., whose need for flexible staffing was not based on production cycles, but rather on completing an overhaul to the company's computer systems infrastructure. Micros Systems designs, manufactures, markets, and supports point-of-sale systems, related peripheral equipment, and software for the hospitality industry. The fast-growing company had to upgrade its information systems in order to handle the requirements of a much larger enterprise. This multi-million-dollar investment necessitated hiring a team of high-level information technology (IT) development professionals, from project managers to programmer/analysts. Robert Moon, director of information systems for Micros Systems, realized that it was not practical to hire a group of IT pros full-time for a project that would take little more than a year. He needed a team of development professionals with very specific skill sets that would not necessarily meet the company's IT needs over the long term. In addition, he needed to assemble a team right away. Moon opted to bring in IT professionals on a contract basis for the system's upgrade. "The project-based, rapidly changing nature of information technology requires flexible staffing methods," Moon explained. "Projects evolve quickly and the skill sets required can change overnight. Bringing in workers on a contract basis provided us with a source of immediate expertise with no lag time for training."[12]

Accounting is yet another example of a profession that is subject to regular workload peaks and valleys. Month-, quarter-, and year-end reporting, tax deadlines, and other busy periods make the field particularly oriented to flexible staffing practices.

FLEXIBLE STAFFING—MAXIMIZING THE PROCESS

These previous examples represent the successful implementation of flexible staffing strategies; but the process goes beyond merely combining a core group of employees with supplemental employees. Companies that embark on this flexible strategy need to do so with care and sensitivity. The strategy must be carefully thought out, and the roles played by workers in each category must be clearly defined.

One of the main reasons that some companies have had trouble implementing this policy is that they continue to use temporary employees in the random, "catch-as-catch-can" manner in which such employees were typically used two decades ago—finding people at the last minute to solve a "crisis" that could have been prevented with some advance planning.

Job security is another issue. The full-time employees or "core staff" in any company using temporary help for peak periods need to have the assurance that the temporaries do not pose a threat to their jobs. Otherwise, productivity will suffer.

And temporary employees, by the same token, need to be treated fairly and communicated with openly and honestly—as members of the team—for optimal results. Companies that have successfully implemented a flexible staffing strategy have set the same standards for temporaries as for full-time workers, and they've made sure that whenever a temporary employee is deployed in a particular capacity, he or she has the necessary skills and training to do the job.

RECRUITING FULL-TIME STAFF FROM TEMPORARY WORKERS

In certain segments of the job market today, as many as 30 percent of temporary assignments become full-time positions. These numbers are not surprising. Many businesses now realize that using temporary employees is actually an effective recruiting tool. It gives companies a way of evaluating the contribution a person can make that is far more reliable than traditional recruiting methods.

TEMPORARY VERSUS FULL-TIME: THE LEGAL DISTINCTION

DANGER!

Now that more companies than ever rely on independent contractors and temporary workers to perform tasks that were once the sole province of regular employees (i.e., employees directly employed by the company), the distinctions that used to differentiate regular employees from independent contractors have begun to blur.

Companies that do not pay careful attention to the distinction between independent contractors and regular employees and that fail to take steps to preserve this distinction leave themselves open to lawsuits and government action. This is particularly true with respect to employment taxes and benefits. For regular employees, employers must withhold the applicable state, federal, and local taxes from the employees' wages and also pay taxes on behalf of the employees. Independent contractors, on the other hand, are responsible for their own tax contributions, and companies using them typically do not withhold any taxes on their behalf.

The definition of employee versus independent contractor is highly subjective and subject to second-guessing by the IRS. Companies that believed they had properly categorized certain workers as independent contractors have learned after the fact that the IRS did not agree with the categorization, resulting in liability for back taxes and penalties on behalf of workers thought to be independent contractors. Companies are well advised to consult legal counsel when using independent contractors.

Increasingly, companies looking to avoid the danger of misclassifying a worker as an independent contractor and the possibility of subsequent liability are turning to specialized staffing firms to obtain highly qualified temporary workers. As the employer of the temporary employee, the staffing firm takes care of workers' compensation and unemployment insurance and local, state, and federal payroll taxes.

THE INS AND OUTS OF OUTSOURCING

Outsourcing is an increasingly common business practice that involves "farming out" to external sources functions that were formerly handled by in-house personnel. This practice has long been common among small businesses, which cannot afford an individual let alone an entire department that specializes in such commonly outsourced functions as advertising, accounting, legal services, or printing. In recent years, large Fortune 500 corporations also have embraced outsourcing, particularly in the management of their complex information technology resources.

Companies typically outsource for one of two reasons: (1) they have determined that it is more economical for them in the long run to farm out a function than to handle the function internally; and (2) they have decided that, costs notwithstanding, outsourcing functions that are not central to their business enables them to concentrate on key operating competencies. Companies outsource, moreover, in the belief that those who perform the outsourced functions, because they specialize, can meet certain needs more effectively and expeditiously.

Andersen Consulting is an example of a firm that has been particularly successful in the information systems (IS) outsourcing market. The company has taken a "one-stop shop" approach to outsourcing, providing its clients with a variety of resources to help them reduce costs and prepare for the future. Andersen Consulting has gone beyond the role of providing traditional outsourcing services, with the formation of research and development laboratories and strategic alliances with industry and academia to provide extra support to clients. The company has also broadened the outsourcing role by working with clients to transform, not just maintain, their IS processes—a critical selling point for clients in today's rapidly changing technological environment. This forward-thinking approach to outsourcing has allowed Andersen Consulting to remain consistently ranked among the world's top IS outsourcing firms.

Then there are other, not-so-successful outsourcing examples. As Gifford and Elizabeth Pinchot remind us in *The Intelligent Organization,* the seminal event in the history of two of the best-known and most powerful companies in the world—Microsoft and Intel—was the day IBM decided to use the consultants as outside sources to hasten IBM's ability to bring the PC to market. As nearly everyone knows, IBM had the capacity in-house to develop the operating system that Microsoft had already developed. It also had the internal ability to produce the central processing unit that was provided by Intel. IBM's rationale at the time was that its own plants and services were too bureaucratic to meet the company's strategic goal of bringing the PC to market.

At first, IBM's outsourcing strategy appeared to be a stroke of operational genius, for within three years, IBM's PC business had grown to more than $4 billion. Eventually, though, IBM found itself losing much of its market to a horde of clones (Compaq, Dell, and others) who had themselves now become big customers of Intel and Microsoft but could bring a competitive product to market at a lower price than IBM. The authors suggest that if IBM had chosen to develop both the operating system and the central processor on its own, it might not have been forced to make the hard changes it made in the late 1980s.[13]

The point here is that outsourcing, valuable as it is, is not always the best alternative to a cumbersome internal system (see Table 3.4). As the Pinchots observe, "Often we need to find a way to do things effectively inside [or internally], not just give up on doing them."

PEOs: VARIATIONS ON THE OUTSOURCING THEME

A professional employer organization (PEO), formerly known as a staff leasing company, is a firm that assumes human resource management responsibility and employer risk on behalf of a client. The client transfers its full-time employees to a PEO, which in turn leases the employees back to the client. Nothing else changes, really. The employees continue to work in the same

TABLE 3.4 OUTSOURCING: PROS AND CONS

Advantages

- Better productivity due to specialization
- Outsourcing company usually has the ability to keep pace with industry advancements and technology
- Less strain on the company's internal administrative support mechanisms

Disadvantages

- Loss of internal control
- Need to reduce permanent staff
- Relying on core competency of others
- Once something is outsourced, it ceases to become a true competitive advantage because other companies can take advantage of the same product or service

capacity as they did before, and continue to be managed by the original employer (now client). The only difference is that their salaries, health insurance, and other benefits are paid for by the PEO, which also handles all the employee-related paperwork, such as filing taxes and workers' compensation premiums. Clients reimburse the PEO for whatever money is paid to the leased employees in the way of salaries and benefits, and also pay a commission based on several factors including the company's gross payroll, its industry, its size, and the breadth of employee benefits and services provided.

PEOs offer companies the potential to receive two direct benefits, one financial and the other administrative. Because PEOs can pool large groups of workers into a single group, they are theoretically able to strike better deals with health insurance companies than smaller organizations, and can thus enable small business owners to provide their employees with benefits that are more attractive and less expensive than would otherwise be the case. This pooling of employees can be particularly beneficial when it comes to reducing workers' compensation insurance costs. Another inducement to many companies is convenience—the fact that PEOs typically handle all the administrative work normally associated with payroll and benefits administration. To date, PEO services have appealed primarily to small businesses with 20 or fewer employees. Current estimates are that PEOs manage approximately 2 million worksite employees representing annual payrolls of $18 billion.

The PEO business has experienced strong growth during the last several years, expanding from a total of 38 firms in 1984 to more than 2400 in 1996. Over the course of its brief history, the industry has had its share of growing pains, however, including isolated instances of malfeasance by a few disreputable firms (see Table 3.5 for ways to check the reliability of a PEO). Fifteen states currently regulate or license PEOs and the industry's association is promoting higher ethical standards by its members.[14]

Stellar Performer: 3M Corporation

Like most major companies, 3M has undergone extensive reengineering over the past 10 years, and during the process has found it necessary to either eliminate entirely or consolidate positions. But instead of laying off those employees whose jobs have been eliminated, 3M has created an internal system that puts these employees on an "unassigned" list and gives them the first chance at interviewing for any open positions that become available in any other unit throughout the company.

According to a report in *Personnel Journal,* 70 percent of the 3M employees who were put on the unassigned list since 1985 have found another full-time job in the company. Of the 30 percent who haven't, many have chosen to accept financial settlements within the first four months of being put on the list and pursue other interests outside the company. Only a few have been terminated after failing to connect with an internal position within six months.

With this system in place, 3M has managed to grow its business, consistently bring in new people, and protect the jobs of those already employed. During the recession of the early 1990s, for example, 3M avoided making the large cutbacks in its workforce that other major employers were forced to do. The effect has been high productivity and less than 3 percent turnover within the salaried workforce.[15]

TABLE 3.5 EIGHT WAYS TO CHECK THE RELIABILITY OF A PEO

- Get credit references from the company's bank.
- Get the name—and check into the reputation—of the company's insurance broker.
- Get detailed information about the company's workers' compensation policies as well as medical and other benefit plans.
- Make sure the company has a reinsurance policy (this arrangement offers protection if a company's limits are exceeded).
- Get the names of and personally speak to other clients. Ask, in particular, about the PEO's responsiveness and promptness.
- Have the company specify, in writing, what specific services it will provide and how much these services will cost.
- Find out whether the company has been audited by an independent party and ask to see the audit.

Adapted from: Tad Shannon, "Searching? Ask the right questions," Eugene, Oregon Register Guard, November 20, 1995.

END POINT

Strategic staffing is a new approach to hiring, built around the premise that hiring decisions must always mirror the short- and long-term goals of the business. Such an approach has become essential for companies that want to remain competitive.

A key aspect to strategic staffing is the judicious use of temporary employees in conjunction with core staff. Two factors are fueling the trend. One is the growing need today for companies to be more flexible in their hiring strategies. The other is the changing makeup of the temporary workforce, which has become increasingly professional, as more and more specialists choose to pursue temporary work as a short- or long-term career strategy.

The principal benefit to companies that adopt this strategy, apart from cost savings, is that they can avoid a vicious cycle of hirings and layoffs. Other benefits include enhanced productivity and the opportunity to use temporary employment as a recruiting method, thereby ensuring that new hires have been "screened." It is, however, important that companies think through their contingent staffing strategies to ensure that the combination of full-time workers and temporaries works smoothly.

Other important trends in strategic staffing today include outsourcing—assigning to outside contractors functions and tasks that are impractical to handle internally—and employee leasing, in which companies assign to an outside source all the administrative and payroll tasks, workers' compensation, and so on. Each of these variations of strategic staffing shows every indication of increasing in years to come as companies move away from the traditional one person per full-time job model. It is, however, essential that companies make sure that they are implementing these policies in a manner that is consistent with strategic objectives and corporate philosophy.

MORE READING

Bennett, Linda J. "The First Step in Complying with the ADA. [Americans with Disabilities Act of 1990]." *Supervisory Management* (April 1993).

Challenger, James E. "Two or More for One: A New Trend in the Workplace." *Manage* (April 1993).

Cronin, Michael P. "Choosing Job-Description Software." *Inc.* (February 1993).

Degner, Jim. "Writing Job Descriptions that Work." *Credit Union Executive* (November/December 1995).

Dunn, Richard. "Titles Are for the Old Country." *Plant Engineering* (July 1996, vol. 50, no. 8), p. 11(1).

Jenks, James M. *The Hiring, Firing (and Everything in Between) Personnel Forms Book.* Ridgefield, Connecticut: Round Lake Publishing, 1992.

Petzinger, Thomas Jr. "Cisco's Staff Conquers Separation Anxieties After Losing Desks." *Wall Street Journal* (February 21, 1997).

Renn, Robert W. and Robert J. Vandenberg. “The Critical Psychological States: An Underrepresented Component in Job Characteristics Model Research.” *Journal of Management* (Summer 1995, vol. 21, no. 2), p. 279(25).

Rittner, Barbara. “Building in Flexibility.” *HR Focus* (October 1996, vol. 73, no. 10), p. 15(2), Reference # A18901622.

CHAPTER 4

Getting the Word Out: The Basics of Effective Recruiting

INTRODUCTION

Recruiting, the process of identifying and attracting qualified job candidates to fill business needs, has evolved considerably in recent years. Today there are more ways of going about it than ever before. But the rationale behind paying attention to recruiting—and doing it well—is the same, regardless of how the process is carried out.

In the past, recruiting was generally considered to be a "personnel" or "human resources" function. The role of line managers in the process was to outline needs at the beginning of the process and then review the final candidates. This division of labor still exists in some organizations. More and more, though, as companies become more decentralized and as smaller companies become the prime engine for job growth, the nuts and bolts of the recruiting process have become the responsibility of business owners and line managers themselves.

And many people are discovering that there is much more to effective recruiting than meets the eye. There is a wide variety of options—classified advertising, job posting, networking, professional recruiters, and so on—and not every option is appropriate in every situation. Above all, though, the recruiting process needs to be well thought out and well planned, and it must be tailored to each individual staffing need. Handled in this manner, recruiting can go a long way toward (1) expanding the number of people considered for a particular job; and (2) streamlining the screening process. But when recruiting is mishandled or taken for granted, the hiring process suffers: It becomes more expensive and more cumbersome and, worse yet, a major potential drain on the company.

This chapter looks at the various avenues companies can take when recruiting and offers insights into how this critical component of the hiring process is best approached.

IT'S NOT A MATTER OF "RIGHT WAY" OR "WRONG WAY"

There is no one "best" way to recruit. Each of the recruiting options described in this chapter (see Table 4.1) is useful, and all deserve thought and consideration. No option, however, is appropriate for every situation, and choosing the best avenues generally depends on a combination of the following factors.

- The strategic and operational importance of the job being filled and the urgency of the need
- The current state of the labor market with respect to the skills and background needed to perform the job
- The nature of the company doing the hiring—its size, culture, and operating style
- In-house recruiting resources—the money, time, and expertise available to spend on the recruiting process

In a well-planned, well-executed recruiting effort, decisions involving what recruiting method to use and how to implement that method should take all of these factors into account. Generally speaking, for instance, the more important the position and the more urgent the need, the more aggressive a company needs to be in its recruiting efforts. But the aggressiveness needs to be controlled. If a classified ad in the local paper fails to generate interest among enough qualified candidates, the answer

TABLE 4.1 RECRUITING OPTIONS AT A GLANCE

The following list shows the 12 most common recruiting methods.

- Recruiting from within the company (i.e., job posting)
- Employee referrals
- Networking among colleagues, vendors, and business associates
- Classified ads (in trade magazines, local newspapers, and national publications such as *The Wall Street Journal, National Business Employment Weekly,* and *The New York Times'* national edition)
- Contingency recruiters
- Executive search firms
- Professional associations (many have job lines and newsletters that list job openings)
- Local, state, and federal employment agencies
- On-line recruiting services and Web site job postings
- College recruiting and internship programs
- Special events, such as open houses
- Temporary services or staffing firms (which provide "temp-to-hire" candidates)

isn't necessarily to rewrite or enlarge the ad or change the advertising medium. The answer might well be to adopt another recruiting method or, in some cases, to rethink the job itself.

Other factors that need to be considered are cost and time. Getting the most out of the process in many situations—particularly when the position is critical and there is not an obvious supply of qualified candidates—can be expensive and enormously time consuming. And managers and business owners who are looking for key people frequently find themselves in the position of having to choose between handling the routine tasks of recruiting themselves or paying an outside specialist to do it.

The point to bear in mind is that the effectiveness of a recruiting effort is ultimately gauged by the results—the number of qualified candidates measured against the time and expense that went into attracting those candidates. The bottom line: If one particular approach to recruiting isn't producing the results, companies need to be willing to explore new options, even if it means breaking with old recruiting traditions.

THE FIRST PLACE TO RECRUIT IS INSIDE THE COMPANY

Companies blessed with loyal customers, high productivity, high morale, and low turnover rates may differ in how they do a lot of things, but virtually all of them share one critical characteristic: They're all committed to a policy of hiring and promoting from within. As a result, the recruiting process in these companies for most jobs other than entry-level positions is directed primarily toward people who are already working for the company.

The rationale for such a policy is sound. Recruiting from within is usually the fastest, most efficient, and least expensive method of assembling a pool of qualified candidates. Internal recruiting generally ensures that the new person in the position will be familiar (and comfortable) with the company's culture, practices, policies, and idiosyncrasies. Internal recruiting minimizes the time it would otherwise take to train and bring newly hired individuals up to speed in a particular job. Most important, perhaps, recruiting from within the company sends an important message to employees: It tells them that if they work hard and do a good job, the company will recognize their contributions, too, and reward them with the opportunity to move their careers forward.

Examples from successful companies abound. When the Gannett Corporation began staffing up for *USA Today* in the early 1980s, it drew its core start-up staff from reporters, editors, and ad salespeople who were already working for other Gannett newspapers across the country.[1] At Marriott Corporation—a company long known for its unusually loyal workforce—some 30 percent of managers began with the company as hourly employees. At Domino's Pizza, based in Ann Arbor, Michigan, 98 percent of the franchisees nationwide are former employees.[2] And at the brokerage firm of A. G. Edwards, where the nine-person executive committee has an average tenure of more than 25 years, 90 to 95 percent of all positions above entry level have always been filled from within the company.[3]

Not that there isn't a downside to internal recruiting. Companies that rely too much on internal sources for their staffing needs run the danger, for example, of becoming too inbred and single-minded—unable to adapt to changing times. It often happens, too, that transferring an employee from one position to another in the company creates problems for the department or the manager that is losing the employee taking on the new assignment. Indeed, one of the ongoing problems for large companies that have extensive job-posting systems is dealing with managers who, for selfish reasons, don't want to part with the employee who wants to move up the ladder.

All of which means that if a company is going to look within its own ranks to fill new positions, it needs to have an organizational structure and a culture that will allow internal recruiting to take place without disrupting operations or producing too many ruffled feathers. Moreover, if internal recruiting is to yield productive results, there needs to be a reasonable supply of employees who are not only qualified for the new position, but are interested in it and eager to stay and grow with the company.

Companies that want to reap the many advantages of recruiting from within must be prepared to deal with the operational and emotional fallout that this practice can bring (see Table 4.2). They also must be ready to invest the time, the effort, and the money required to develop employees and keep them motivated. As Frederick Reichheld points out in the *The Loyalty Effect,* companies known for their stable, productive workforces not only are rigorous in their hiring procedures (they hire only a fraction of the applicants who actually apply), they also go to great lengths to train and develop newly hired personnel. Furthermore, they have instituted compensation and bonus incentives that make it well worth employees' while to stay with the company.[4]

TABLE 4.2 MINIMIZING THE PROBLEMS THAT INTERNAL RECRUITING CAN SOMETIMES CREATE

Any company that intends to rely mainly on its internal resources to fill new jobs needs to develop a coherent and consistent set of policies that address the following issues.

- What mechanism will be used to keep employees informed of job openings as they arise, and what safeguards are in place to make sure that everyone is given an equal opportunity to apply for jobs that they feel they are qualified to fill?
- What role, if any, will be played in the process by the person currently supervising an employee who is interested in applying for another job? And how does a company ensure that the supervisor who doesn't want to see the employee take on the new job (for selfish reasons) doesn't subvert the process?
- How does the company balance its ongoing operational needs with the aspirations of employees whose rise to a higher position could create a temporary disruption in the day-to-day work of the business?

State Farm Insurance is a classic example. The company's process for hiring new agents was once likened by *Fortune Magazine* to the process somebody might go through to choose a spouse. But those rigorous policies are only the tip of the iceberg. Newly hired sales personnel at State Farm, according to Reichheld, typically undergo anywhere from two to three years of training before they become eligible to be agents. And once they become agents, they join a system in which there is great deal of internal support and a direct connection between job performance and compensation.

State Farm has yet another practice that deviates from the norm, but nonetheless motivates its employees. The company knows that most of its agents, once they've been assigned a territory, will want to stay with that territory, rather than move around from one part of the country to another, and will also want to remain in sales, as opposed to moving into management positions. So it has structured its business around that principle. Agents who have a desire to move into management can do so, but there are no real financial incentives or institutional peer pressure to make the move. At State Farm, an administrator who rises to become president of the company will make only a "fraction of what the top agents earn."

The key point here is the interconnectedness of all the policies. The State Farm example, along with the hundreds of other examples that could be cited from successful companies, demonstrates clearly that recruiting from within is a great policy to follow, but only if everything else a company provides (i.e., the structure and the environment) allows this policy to flourish.[5]

BE WILLING TO TAKE A CHANCE

Companies committed to the practice of using homegrown talent to fuel their growth must be prepared to show faith in their employees and to take chances on employees who do not necessarily meet all the hiring criteria that have been established for any given position. The key in these instances is twofold: (1) the employee's experience needs to be close enough to the criteria so that he or she won't be overwhelmed by the new position; and (2) the employee needs to be motivated to do whatever it takes to meet the new challenge.

One small company that has succeeded at this balancing act is Fitcorp, Inc. Fitcorp runs fitness centers for businesses in the Boston area, and has an ongoing need for center directors who not only have experience in exercise physiology but also have strong management and people skills. Nearly 80 percent of all Fitcorp employees started out as student interns, and more than 95 percent of the company's center directors are homegrown. But those numbers wouldn't be that high had the company not been willing to let its newly promoted directors "grow" into the job.[6]

TURNING EMPLOYEES INTO RECRUITERS

One of the most effective methods of recruiting also happens to be one of the simplest and least expensive. It's the familiar practice of networking—getting informal networks (employees,

Stellar Performer: AMP Inc.
Job Posting by Phone

A growing sense of employee dissatisfaction toward internal recruiting policies led AMP Inc., the world's largest manufacturer of electrical and electronic connections, to completely revamp its long-standing job-posting policies in the early 1990s. The process AMP went through represents a good case study on bringing a cumbersome and antiquated internal recruiting program up to date.

The Harrisburg, Pennsylvania–based company had been using the same internal recruiting policies since the mid-1940s. It was a mixed bag of bulletin-board postings, supplemented by an internal database that was ostensibly designed to help supervisors find existing employees who met the hiring criteria for specific jobs. Workers identified their career aspirations in written form, and their responses became part of a database that hiring managers could use when they were looking for new people—if they were of a mind to do so.

This policy worked well enough when the company was relatively small, but with 15,000 employees, AMP's system of job policies was creating a variety of problems with which most large companies should be able to identify.

- The form that employees filled out was limited to only three career choices.
- Employees were frequently unaware of openings until the openings were filled.
- Supervisors were under no obligation to inform their direct reports that they were being considered for open positions.
- There was no mechanism for feedback when employees who applied for jobs were turned down.
- Some of the business units refused to allow their employees to be considered for openings.
- Supervisors and managers of employees who participated in the original in-house recruitment program automatically assumed the employees were unhappy with their current positions.
- Employees who wanted to use the program feared reprisal from current supervisors.

(Continued)

(Continued)

- The process overall was extremely cumbersome, creating a tremendous amount of paperwork.

AMP's answer to these problems was to create a job-posting team charged with replacing the current system with one that would get information to employees in the fastest, most efficient way. The traditional bulletin-board job-posting system was ruled out because it was too unwieldy and slow. Computers were ruled out because only 20 percent of AMP's employees had computers at the time. This left one option: a phone-based information system that would enable employees to call a central number 24 hours a day and receive information on all the job opportunities that were currently available in the company.

The system works as follows. Once the human resources department receives an "employment requisition," that requisition is entered into the system, at which point someone makes a job announcement on the company's voice mail system. Employees interested in learning about openings can call an in-house extension or an outside toll-free number to learn of the openings. Callers are asked to select from a series of prompts that ultimately lead to a specific "mailbox" where they can hear of all the job openings that relate to a specific category such as geographical area, or some functional area such as sales or administration. The system enables callers to respond to as many or as few openings as they like by simply transferring to a separate response mailbox, where they leave certain basic information: name, employee number, job number, and supervisor's name. The responses are retrieved daily and tracked; after seven days, all the responses are entered into the system, which automatically generates an "employee profile sheet" for each respondent. The sheet eventually finds its way to a human resources representative, who reviews the data with the hiring supervisor and arranges interviews. Once the interview is over, the hiring manager's feedback is programmed into the computer, which then generates a letter containing the feedback to each candidate.

So much for the nuts and bolts of the system. Elegant though the program was, the job-posting team still had to get buy-in not only

(Continued)

(Continued)

from the supervisors, but also from the top-level executive planning committee consisting of the president, chief executive officer, and other key direct reports. That buy-in came, but not without the willingness of the team to make modifications that eased the concerns of supervisors. In any event, the system was ultimately implemented in 1992, and, according to the company, has been a success. [7]

Employees like the system for the following reasons.

- The toll-free number provides flexibility that allows employees to call from home or even while they're on vacation.
- The system easily provides information on available jobs.
- It's fair: Everyone has equal access to the information.
- Over the long term, the company saw a 16 percent decrease in the number of days positions stayed open.

friends, contacts, colleagues, vendors, etc.) to spread the word about a company's staffing needs and to be on the lookout for likely candidates. Probably the most common form of networking as a recruiting strategy is an employee referral program through which employees who bring new employees into the company are rewarded in some way: money, dinner, or a day off, for example (see Table 4.3). Employee referral programs have been on the increase over the past few years now that companies in more and more industries are having trouble attracting qualified employees through conventional methods.

Amica Mutual Insurance, a Providence, Rhode Island-based insurance company that enjoys one of the highest customer satisfaction ratings in the insurance business, relies primarily on referrals from existing employees, offering a series of attractive incentives to employees who recommend candidates who are eventually hired.[8] There is, of course, one catch. Regardless of the incentive, employee referral programs only work if the employees are reasonably happy in their jobs.

TABLE 4.3 MAKING REFERRALS WORTHWHILE

Nearly all employee referral programs offer incentives. Here's a list of the most common:

- Money—anywhere from $50 to $5000, depending on the importance of the position and how tight the labor market is for that position
- Time off or added vacation time
- Dinner at a local restaurant
- Employee's name on a plaque or similar recognition
- A group lunch or dinner with the company president

Employee referral programs need to be well thought out, with special attention given to the following issues.

- What's the minimum amount of time an employee who has been referred needs to stay on the payroll before the incentive kicks in? (The usual practice is between four and six months.)
- What is the actual recommendation procedure? (At the very least, there should be a written or computerized form that allows a company to track the source of each referral and its outcome.)
- What happens when two or more employees recommend the same candidate?

RECRUITING FRIENDS AND FAMILY MEMBERS IS NOT NECESSARILY A BAD THING

Although many companies today strive to create a sense of "family" among employees, most have traditionally been uncomfortable with the idea of having too many employees who are actually related to one another. Some companies, in fact, have policies that specifically forbid people in the same family to work in the same department or company.

There's no arguing that the personal relationships and the family connections among people could have a disruptive effect on a company's ability to operate efficiently. How do you prevent favoritism? And what happens when family frictions spill over in the workplace?

These concerns notwithstanding, many of the companies that have been singled out in the business press over the past several years for their outstanding levels of productivity and morale don't seem to be the least bit concerned about having friends and relatives working side by side. Nearly 7 percent of the workforce at Southwest Airlines, for instance, consists of married couples. And at Quad/Graphics, a billion-dollar printing company based in Wisconsin, some 4900 of the 8500 employees are related by either blood or marriage.[9]

Companies that encourage their employees to recruit family members and friends defend the practice on the following basis.

- Certain traits that are important in the workforce—honesty, a strong work ethic, and the like—tend to run in families.
- Good employees will be reluctant to recommend family members (or anyone, for that matter) who might become a source of embarrassment to them or the company.
- The possibility of the quality of work suffering because of friction is outweighed by the positive effects of a strong family feeling.
- People working in companies with people they know well or are related to are much less likely than others to go to another company.

When brothers Bob and Dave Asch set up their company, Twincraft Soap, they had heard many stories about other family businesses destroyed by nepotism. They were so concerned that nepotism could be the undoing of their business that they crafted a family employment policy to ensure the survival of Twincraft. The policy stands as a model for other businesses run by families, or for those who hire a number of employees from the same family.

Firmly rooted in "tough love," the basic premise of the policy is this: "No protectionism or undue privileges" for family members. Adherence to the policy is overseen by a group of nonfamily managers. Additionally, in order to work for the company, family members must have previous experience and must go through an impartial interview, and may not take a manager's position unless they have had three years of related experience at another company.

Further, when it comes to raises and promotions, family members are rated alongside nonfamily members.

Employees of Twincraft (family and nonfamily alike) are quite happy with the policy, and no one feels taken advantage of.[10]

Table 4.4 shows turnover rates for employees recruited by different methods.

CLASSIFIED INFORMATION: HOW TO WRITE BETTER RECRUITMENT ADS

Placing classified ads in newspapers and other publications is probably the most widely used recruiting method in America, but few hiring professionals would describe the method as the most effective. The big drawback with classified ads is that people who are currently working and are happy in their jobs don't tend to read them,

TABLE 4.4 REFERRAL METHODS AND TURNOVER: A COMPARATIVE LOOK

When the consulting firm Bain & Company conducted a survey of a large brokerage firm that was seeking to cut down on employee turnover, it found that first-year turnover rates were the most favorable among candidates who had been referred by employees and the least favorable among brokers who'd been recruited from the competition.

The numbers were as follows, based on percentage of new hires who left the company after one year.

- Referred by other employees: 30 percent
- College recruits: 45 percent
- Responded to newspaper ads: 55 percent
- Recruited from the competition: 67 percent[11]

Stellar Performer
How One Company Spreads the Word

It is common practice among senior managers and business owners to be on the lookout for people who might make good employees—even when there isn't a current opening. But a Dallas-based food broker named Luke Soules Southwest has added an imaginative new dimension to this practice. The company refers to this version of networking practice as creating "centers of influence." The idea, in short, is to create a veritable army of outside people who are themselves on the lookout for people who would make good Luke Soules Southwest employees.

The company's methodology, according to its president, Tom Garrison, couldn't be more direct or open. Whenever Garrison comes across someone (on a shopping trip, for example) that he thinks would make a good employee, he engages that person in conversation, tells the person a little about his business and his company, and tries to interest the person in coming to work for Luke Soules Southwest someday.

But he doesn't stop there. Even if the person isn't interested, Garrison will ask this "newly minted center of influence" to be on the lookout for people who might fit the ideal candidate description that they have been talking about. Garrison told *Inc.* magazine in the early 1990s that after he and his retail managers had been "seeding" the Dallas area with centers of influence for six years, the company was getting four or five calls a week from potential candidates.[12]

which means the ads are reaching a limited segment of the people who are ideally qualified for a position.

This reservation aside, classified advertising can still be a productive recruiting strategy—particularly for entry-level and mid-level jobs. The strategy, however, needs to be thoughtfully implemented, and anyone using this method needs to recognize that getting good results from classified advertising involves more than simply throwing some words together and placing an ad in the local paper (see Table 4.5). Where the ad is placed, what the headline says, how large it is, the wording of the ad itself—each of these factors can affect not only the number of responses the ad draws but the quality of those responses: the percentage of respondents who are worth taking a closer look at.

The difference between the *quantity* and the *quality* of the response deserves elaboration. The ultimate purpose of a recruitment ad, remember, is not simply to draw the largest number of responses. It is to draw a significant number of responses from people who are worth interviewing.

THE ANATOMY OF AN EFFECTIVE RECRUITMENT AD

If an ad is to attract the interest of candidates who are genuinely qualified for the position, it should do the following.

- Give the reader a broad idea of the position and the general nature of the company (its size, business, location, etc.)
- Indicate the key elements of the job description and the qualifications required
- Give a general idea of the company culture, thus weeding out some of the people who should not be applying

Note: Remember that all advertisements should comply with federal and state equal opportunity employment laws.

TABLE 4.5 FOUR SUGGESTIONS FOR GETTING MORE OUT OF CLASSIFIED RECRUITING

1. *Choose the media with care.* The majority of classified ads that companies place on any given day in the United States appear in metropolitan areas because of their large circulation and readers' commuting distance. Frequently, however, a company would be well advised to expand the scope of its campaign. The key factors are (1) the proportion of the circulation likely to be interested in the position and (2) the cost of the ad. Possibilities to consider include the following.
   - Local community newspapers (a good source for part-time administrative professionals)
   - National newspapers, such as *The New York Times'* national edition, *The Wall Street Journal,* and *National Business Employment Weekly*
   - Classified sections of professional and trade publications
2. *Think twice about using "blind" ads.* One of the choices a company needs to make when running a classified ad is whether to identify itself in the ad or run a "blind" ad—one that gives only the box number as a response option. The main rationale for running a blind ad is that a company doesn't want to advertise the fact (particularly to its current employees) that it is actively looking to fill a particular job. The downside: Blind ads tend to discourage responses from people who are currently working but understandably reluctant to write a response to an ad that could end up on the desk of their current employer. Best rule of thumb: Unless there's a strong reason for not doing so, companies are better off identifying who they are.
3. *Communicate company values.* Steve Kantor, president of Gnossos Software in Washington, DC, wrote an ad recently that brought five times more responses than the newspaper had told him to expect—about 175 in all—and turned up five finalists he would have been more than happy to hire. The ad began, "Small entrepreneurial firm seeks sharp liberal arts grad. Vision, ethics, personality required." Kantor claims many of the candidates cited "ethics" as the reason they answered the ad.[13]
4. *Give thought to response mechanisms.* How you ask candidates to reply to an ad could go a long way in determining how many responses you receive and how much time company employees will spend answering the calls from candidates who are clearly unqualified. In general, the more hoops a person reading an ad is asked to jump through, the fewer responses the ad is likely to draw. On the flip side, however, those responses will come from candidates who are genuinely interested.

- Spell out anything special that would make the job attractive to certain qualified people (flex hours, convenient location, attractive surroundings, etc.)
- Create excitement—communicate the attractiveness of the job without painting a misleading picture

Here are some examples.

MUSIC: MANAGING EDITOR

Leading international print music publisher located in Chicago seeks Managing Editor to coordinate the process from manuscript to printed edition. Responsibilities incl. editing of submitted material for all genres of music & direct engravers, proofreaders, and outside editors. Must have in-depth knowledge of publishing practices & procedures. Extensive exp req'd coupled with impeccable knowledge of the music craft. Competitive sal & exc benefits package. Fax resume with salary history in confidence.

OFFICE MANAGER, AD AGENCY

Small ad agency known for its creativity seeks office manager who is a self-starter who pays attention to details and deadlines. Main duties: bookkeeping, scheduling, and routine correspondence. Attractive offices in downtown Chicago. Competitive salary and generous benefits for the right person.

MARKET RESEARCH, SENIOR PROJECT DIRECTOR

If you are a market research expert, we want you as our Sr. Director of market research. We are a mid-sized (40 employees) market research company located in San Jose, and we are in need of an accomplished professional with strong writing skills to manage quantitative and qualitative research projects, from analysis to final reporting. Must be able to direct and supervise the efforts of research and project associates, write proposals, develop research design, methods and sample size and direct on-line searches to demonstrate understanding of business issues. Focus group moderating experience a plus. Must have advanced degree. Submit writing samples and resume to:

OUTSIDE SALES REP, CONSULTING SERVICES
We need a polished pro (at least five years bus. to bus. selling experience) with proven ability to sell big ticket technical consulting services. Ours is a demanding, performance-oriented corporate culture, but there is excellent income if you can handle the pressure. Technical background a big plus.

These ads differ in many respects. The first two are written in a relatively formal style. The third and fourth are more casual—note the stronger reliance on personal pronouns. The ads also differ in length and in emphasis. Fundamentally, though, all meet the criteria described above. They offer an overview of the job and indicate what qualities are necessary to do the job well. Pay especially close attention to how specific the language is in both cases. There is little or no hype, simply an accurate description of what the job involves. Note, too, that each of the ads, either explicitly or implicitly, gives readers a sense of the company culture.

True, two of the ads are fairly long, and not all companies can afford to spend the extra money that lengthy ads can cost. But as the shorter examples show, it's still possible to write an effective ad in four or five lines.

OUTSIDE HELP: GETTING THE MOST OUT OF PROFESSIONAL RECRUITERS

Tens of thousands of companies throughout the world are in the recruiting business. They specialize in helping organizations attract and screen job candidates. They have long played an important role in the hiring process for companies of every size and in virtually every industry.

The recruiting industry is made up of different types of specialists, but nearly all fall into one of two categories: recruitment or contingency search firms (also known as employment agencies) and executive search firms. Both types of companies locate and screen candidates, and eventually recommend the top contenders to their clients. The difference lies mainly in the types of job searches the firms specialize in and in how they charge (see Table 4.6). Contingency recruiters, those that collect fees only when they successfully place a job candidate, generally focus on staff- to managerial-level positions, but may also search for executives earning as much as $150,000. Executive search firms specialize in narrower, higher-level searches, but may also look for less senior personnel. While there is some overlap, each takes a different approach: Contingency firms tend to rely on advertising, their own candidate databases, and industry contacts, while executive search firms depend largely on networking.

TABLE 4.6 HOW RECRUITERS DIFFER

Recruitment (or contingency search) firms and executive search firms share certain functions in common, but here are the principal differences.

Recruitment (or Contingency Search) Firms

- Work on a contingent basis only—paid if and when a candidate is hired
- Focus on (with certain exceptions) staff to managerial level jobs
- Have an existing database of job seekers who have registered with them
- Rely on advertising, their own candidate database, and networking to find candidates
- Charge fees in the range of 30 percent of the candidate's first-year salary
- Frequently provide replacement guarantees

Executive Search Firms

- Typically charge one-third of candidate's first-year compensation, plus expenses
- Are paid a retainer fee, whether or not a candidate is hired
- Specialize in higher-level professional searches (minimum salary for the job is usually $100,000 a year)
- Rely mainly on networking to uncover candidates

Professional recruitment firms are usually able to handle all the various phases of recruiting in a more efficient and more timely manner than the average company. They know how to get the most out of classified advertising and are skilled at weeding out unqualified candidates. Through testing procedures or in-depth interviewing, they can provide an accurate picture of a candidate's technical skills. They have systematic ways of checking out references. Many recruitment firms can also be helpful in advising clients on how to structure a compensation package and how to rethink staffing strategies when companies are having trouble filling positions. A number of these firms specialize in particular occupations, which can make it easier for companies to communicate their needs and can ultimately increase the prospects of a better match.

All in all, recruitment firms offer two key benefits: (1) they provide access to qualified candidates that client companies might not have been able to tap; and (2) they assume the burden of recruiting tasks that client companies may not excel at or may not have the time to handle themselves.

However, one major consideration is cost. Companies need to weigh the cost of using outside recruiting against two factors. The first is the time and resources that would be consumed if recruiting were handled internally. Candidate screening efforts alone can be both costly and time consuming. Findings from a recent study by the Saratoga Institute reported in the *Staffing Industry Report* of July 31, 1997, showed that the average cost for companies to hire an external exempt employee climbed to $8512 in 1996. Companies that are less experienced in conducting internal recruiting efforts may absorb even further costs. The second factor is the competitive edge a company stands to lose if it fails to fill a key position in a timely manner. (This is not to mention the cost and disruption that result when ineffective internal recruiting practices fail to produce a candidate who is genuinely qualified to fill the position.) Companies also have to factor in the likelihood of attracting a better crop of candidates. The recruiting industry as a whole has become more specialized over the past 20 years. Now, the larger staffing firms also provide a wide range of value-added services that go beyond the normal parameters of recruiting. Performance standards are high: Companies that can't keep commitments or give clients what they want are no longer able to compete. Replacement guarantees are usually provided by leading recruitment firms.

KEY CONCEPT

MAKING THE RIGHT CHOICE

Deciding which recruiter to use for any particular assignment requires the same level of research that would go into choosing any other professional services vendor for the company. The more targeted and comprehensive the research, the more likely it is that the choice will be successful. The most important consideration—apart from the general ethical standards of the firm—is the recruiter's expertise and track record in those areas that relate directly to the position being filled (see Table 4.7). Some specific things to do when evaluating a recruiter include the following.

- Visit the recruiter's office personally and make sure the atmosphere reflects professionalism and integrity.
- Get references—particularly among companies with similar staffing needs.

TABLE 4.7 NINE IMPORTANT THINGS TO FIND OUT ABOUT A RECRUITER

- Who owns and manages the firm?
- How long has it been in business?
- What industries or areas (if any) does it specialize in?
- Who are its clients?
- How does it recruit and screen applicants?
- Which person in the office will actually be handling the account?
- What are the fee arrangements?
- Can the recruiter extend its search beyond the local market?
- What sort of a replacement guarantee does the company offer in the event a candidate is hired but doesn't work out?

- Find out about screening policies (i.e., application forms, and specific methods that are used to ascertain candidate skill levels).
- Look for a proven track record or expertise in your industry or specific occupational category.
- Meet and interview the person or people who will actually be conducting the search, and ask for references.
- Clarify the fee arrangements in writing.

Avoid entirely—or be exceptionally wary of—any recruiter or recruitment firm that:

- Is evasive or reluctant about giving out client reference information
- Is difficult to reach or uncommunicative
- Charges candidates for its services (including the preparation of resumes)
- Uses high-pressure techniques
- Won't keep you posted on the progress of the search
- Has been in the recruiting business for only a short time or lacks a successful track record

INTERNET RECRUITING: NEW TOOL IN THE HIRING ARSENAL

Now that tens of millions of people throughout the world are accessing information and communicating with one another via the Internet, it's no surprise that companies in increasing numbers are integrating on-line programs into their overall recruiting efforts. The strategies include the following.

1. *Capitalizing on their own Web sites:* Job descriptions and listings are available on many corporate Web sites. These sites usually are registered with all of the major search engines—Yahoo, Excite, Infoseek, and AltaVista, for example. Candidates frequently use these search engines to look for specific positions and companies.

2. *Using on-line career centers to advertise available positions:* Career centers include large all-purpose services, such as CareerMosaic, Monster Board, and Intellimatch, which, in addition to job listings, also offer career and networking tips (see Table 4.8). These Web sites store candidates' resumes in searchable databases, and many offer "matching services," in which a company submits a job request and the career center responds with six or seven resumes that match the request. These sites can be accessed by using an Internet service provider (ISP), including commercial on-line services such as America Online or Microsoft Network. (The commercial services are ISPs that provide unique content in addition to e-mail and Internet access, whereas ISPs such as AT&T Wordnet, Netcome Inc., and GTE Intelligent Network Services generally provide only Internet access and e-mail.)
3. *Accessing newsgroups to network and publicize positions:* UseNet newsgroups are like large bulletin boards and are visited by millions of people every day. Companies can post job listings at alt.jobs, misc.jobs, and biz.jobs.offered, for example, or they can regularly monitor these and other newsgroups as a tool to search for qualified candidates.

TABLE 4.8 KEY PLAYERS IN THE ON-LINE RECRUITING GAME

- CareerMosaic
- Intellimatch
- Monster Board
- Online Career Center
- CareerPath
- CareerSite
- CareerWEB
- Job Web
- JobTrak
- careers.wsj.com[14]

The percentage of people actually hired after being recruited on-line is still small compared to the millions hired yearly through more conventional channels. Most on-line recruiting occurs in the technical and educational fields. However, the benefits of the emerging market for on-line recruiting include the following.

1. *Cost-effective access to a huge audience:* In contrast to newspaper ads, on-line postings have the potential to reach millions of people—and at a much lower cost (based on circulation) than the typical classified listing. The postings themselves can remain on-line for several weeks or indefinitely.
2. *A targeted, technically savvy audience:* Companies can be reasonably assured that anyone who accesses and responds to an on-line job listing already possesses some basic computer skills—a prerequisite for many jobs today. On-line recruiting won't help companies target geographically, however. Distant candidates applying for local jobs may be a drawback for some firms.
3. *Timelier monitoring capabilities:* On-line postings enable employers to conveniently track responses from moment to moment. Moreover, listings can be easily updated or expanded as needed. On the other hand, postings can result in a large volume of e-mails and resumes, and the time initially saved by recruiting on-line may be consumed by screening such a large number of candidates.
4. *Reduced paperwork:* On-line recruiting generally saves companies time and paperwork when responding to candidate queries. Those individuals whose resumes look promising can be sent e-mail messages, eliminating the need to draft letters or place telephone calls.

The cost of on-line recruiting varies considerably and is in a constant state of flux. Creating a corporate Web site, for example, can cost anywhere from several hundred dollars, assuming you have the internal resources to use off-the-shelf software, to upward of $1 million, depending on who sets up the site, how elaborate it is, and where your firm is located. According to *NetMarketing's* "Web Price Index," Internet development is less expensive in Dallas and Atlanta than in Chicago or San Francisco.[15] In addition, accessing the Internet for the purpose of recruiting can range in price from a monthly membership fee of $20 or $30 to several thousand dollars annually in search fees. Advertising your job listings with career centers could add thousands of dollars annually to the budget of the Internet recruiting program.

In addition to expense, privacy may be another concern for your firm. Job listings can be accessed by anyone at any time. If candidates are asked to e-mail resumes and cover letters, it is critical to establish a secure firewall for protection against technically skilled hackers who could wreak havoc on your company's network.

Table 4.9 offers some pointers on getting started in on-line recruiting.

TABLE 4.9 TAKING THE PLUNGE

Here are four key pieces of advice for companies contemplating an on-line recruiting initiative.

1. *Develop on-line expertise.* The person in the company responsible for on-line recruiting needs to be familiar with Internet technology. Before anyone can take advantage of the specific recruitment services, he or she first needs to master the basics.
2. *Research the market.* Take time to research the various recruitment and job-posting services available on the Internet. Use search engines to get listings of the Web sites that relate to employment. Visit each Web site to assess its fit with your recruiting needs. Additionally, check the Web sites of recruitment firms that specialize in your industry.
3. *Compare costs.* Get specific information about the pricing policy of each site, and make sure the investment makes sense given the scope of the search.
4. *Experiment.* The Internet is in a constant state of change, with new services cropping up at an ever increasing rate. On-line recruiting strategies should continually be reevaluated. Users should be prepared to experiment with (and track) several options to determine which strategy makes the most sense.

INTERNET SEARCHES: NOT A SILVER BULLET

DANGER!

Although Internet searches and employment listings have enabled companies to dramatically broaden the scope of their efforts to attract new candidates, keep in mind that on-line recruiting is a tool and not a panacea. Candidates who emerge through on-line recruiting efforts need to be evaluated as carefully as candidates recruited using more conventional methods, if not more so. For example, screening, including reference checking, cannot be any less diligent.

In addition, Internet recruitment policies may need to be developed internally. Candidates who send resumes via e-mail deserve the same courtesy as those who solicit employment through traditional routes, whether it's a follow-up phone call, a personal note, or a response letter. Ideally, on-line resources should be part of the hiring mix, along with such conventional sources as networking, classified ads, and the other techniques described in this chapter.

COLLEGE RECRUITING: CHANGING OF THE GUARD

Colleges have always been—and will always be—the number one source of entry-level talent for most companies. But the overall college recruiting picture is much different today than it was even 10 years ago. Fewer companies today have the budget or time to handle college recruiting in the grand old way—with frequent visits to campuses, expensive brochures, recruiting videos, open houses for college students, and so forth. At larger firms, the people responsible for recruiting on college campuses are becoming much more targeted, focusing on those schools with strong departments in the specialties they need and concentrating on hiring the top students. Meanwhile, thousands of smaller companies that never did much college recruiting have begun doing so.

But the most important trend these days in college recruiting is the surging number of companies using college students as interns, not only during the summers but during the school year itself. A typical example can found at the Indialantic, Florida, home of a small software company called Software Productivity Solutions (SPS). When SPS begins a new project, it gets in touch with the nearby Florida Institute of Technology, one of the more than 1300 U.S. colleges whose students are currently in internship programs with local companies. Computer science professors send the company president resumes of students, primarily seniors. Students typically work on teams for 20 hours a week at $10 an hour. Afterward, each student is evaluated for SPS, and many are eventually hired as full-time employees.

SPS's internships are highly popular with Florida Institute of Technology students because SPS goes out of its way to make the experience worthwhile. Every intern gets a chance to articulate his or her own goals, and each is paired with a senior engineer who monitors the intern's performance and whose opinion is sought if the intern applies for full-time work.[16]

SPS's successful use of interns typifies why internships are so popular with everyone involved in the process—students, companies, and the colleges and universities who coordinate the programs. Students like the fact that they're getting a realistic taste of what it might be like to work at a particular job or in a particular company. Companies get skilled labor at a relatively inexpensive cost, boost morale by bringing in young people with fresh ideas, and develop good PR at the local colleges. Colleges, for their part, can use these connections with local businesses as ammunition in their own recruiting efforts.

Increasingly, companies are hiring their interns for entry-level positions. Studies show, too, that there is less turnover among those college hires who have been interns than there is among college students overall. And it is estimated that the recruiting and training costs associated with the hiring of interns are half of those for recruiting other employees.

Now for the fine print. Internships have become so popular in recent years that competition for top interns is becoming almost as intense as competition for top graduates. Indeed, most major companies view the internships they offer as a recruiting tactic—a way of gaining the inside track on the top graduates *before* they're actively wooed by other companies. The result is that companies have to do more than ever before to make the internships attractive. The going rate for interns today varies by industry and geographic region, but can range from between $500 and $800 or more a week, with school-year internships including part or all of the tuition for any credit the student will receive. Larger companies sweeten the offer by providing students from out of town with complimentary housing at nearby colleges.[17]

Companies must also be able to make the case that the internship is going to be exciting and worthwhile. The key point to bear in mind: Companies that want to attract the top talent in today's internship sweepstakes have to be willing to play the game by the new rules (see Table 4.10).

DEVELOPING RAPPORT WITH LOCAL COLLEGES

Whether a local college is seen as a prime source of interns or entry-level candidates, it is usually a good idea for companies of all sizes to develop a close working relationship with the college. Here are some suggestions on how to do this.

- Regularly recruit on campus.

TABLE 4.10 FIVE KEYS TO SETTING UP A SUCCESSFUL INTERNSHIP PROGRAM

- Target only those interns who are genuinely interested in the field (as opposed to people looking for a "summer job").
- Take time in the beginning to clarify what the intern wants to gain from the experience.
- Assign a mentor to each intern.
- Create a structured work experience that gives the intern hands-on experience in different phases of the business.
- Make it a goal of the department to ultimately offer a full-time position to the intern.

- Contribute to fundraising campaigns or other university projects.
- Get in touch with the person who heads the targeted department that applies to the position and volunteer to become a visiting lecturer.
- Explore opportunities to recruit from the university's graduate school.
- Have members of the staff apply for jobs as adjunct or visiting professionals.
- Lend support to school activities; for example, by sponsoring a job fair.
- Create a scholarship fund.
- If the college has a career or placement center, establish ongoing contacts.

END POINT

The effectiveness of recruiting, the process of identifying and attracting qualified candidates, is ultimately gauged by the results—the number of suitable candidates that emerge, measured against the time and expense that goes into attracting those prospects.

The key to successful recruiting is that it must be strategically coordinated with the needs of the business, the department, and current conditions in the local labor market. There is a wide variety of recruiting options available today, and no one strategy works best in every situation.

When companies rely on internal recruiting to fill key positions, policies need to be well thought out and supported by adequate training and development practices.

The two most common recruitment strategies, apart from internal recruiting, are classified ads and the use of outside recruiters. The chief downside to classified advertising is that the ads rarely capture the attention of people who are working and satisfied with their jobs. In any case, the ads need to be worded carefully to attract legitimate candidates.

Outside recruiting sources primarily fall into one of two categories: recruitment firms or contin-

Stellar Performer
Back to the Future

Among the more novel ways in which some companies are responding to the shortage of skilled workers today is a new version of a much older and much more traditional approach—apprenticeships. The Max Daetwyler Corporation, a Swiss-owned supplier of printing equipment and products located in Huntersville, North Carolina, is a case in point.

In 1994, shortly after it expanded its product assembly operation and found itself in dire need of qualified workers, Daetwyler joined forces with two other regional companies that were facing similar problems to form an apprenticeship program.

Representatives from the three companies go on recruiting missions to local high schools each spring in search of students who spend a good portion of their senior year working as interns at one of the three firms. Students who are interested visit the company for which they would like to apprentice and complete 20 hours of "job shadowing," working one week, four hours per day.

If all goes well, the students move to the next stage in the program: the "pre-apprenticeship," which consists of on-the-job paid training combined with classroom instruction at a local community college. During this period, participants get a hands-on sense of how good they are at this work and how much they enjoy it. The companies, meantime, get a chance to see whether students have the aptitude for the work. Once the summer is over, students who make the grade are hired for 20 hours per week during their senior year. When the program participants graduate from high school, they are given an opportunity to join the company in which they apprenticed and attend a local college at the same time. (Each company pays college tuition for apprentices.) When the apprenticeship is over, the students end up with associate's degrees in manufacturing engineering technology, as well as apprenticeship certificates from the North Carolina Department of Labor.

What is noteworthy about the program is that there are no contractual obligations. Apprentices who go through the program are under no obligation to stay with the company. The program is too

(Continued)

(Continued)

new to judge its success, but executives are optimistic. The alternative, as Gwen Robert, the company's human resources manager, explained, is to go back to the old way of hiring "people who came without the skills to do the job, that the company was paying $10 per hour, and still having to train them anyway. The idea behind the apprenticeship program is to start them earlier, pay a little less, move them along progressively, and more. We're creating our future workforce."[18]

gency search firms (also known as employment agencies) and executive search firms. The difference lies mainly in the kinds of searches they specialize in and in how they charge. The advantage of using these outside firms is that they employ skilled hiring professionals who are trained in the myriad of issues related to the entire recruitment process.

Colleges continue to be a source of entry-level talent, but are not just limited to potential full-time employees. Many companies are using undergraduate interns to supplement their staff during the school year and the summer.

MORE READING

"A Primer on Screening Job Applicants." *Inc.* (March 1990).

Fenn, Donna. "When Should You Make a Counteroffer?" *Inc.* (July 1996).

Fisher, Roger and William Ury. *Getting to Yes: Negotiating Agreement Without Giving In.* New York: Penguin Books, 1983.

Green, Paul C. *Getting Hired! Winning Strategies to Ace the Interview.* Austin, Texas: Bard Press, 1996.

Levering, Robert and Milton Moskowitz. *The 100 Best Companies to Work For in America.* New York: Penguin Books, 1994.

Overman, Stephenie. "Hiring the Right Stuff." *HR Magazine* (April 1994).

Pape, William R. "Hire Power (Hiring Workers Who Telecommute)." *Inc.* (November 1996).

Spragins, Ellyn. "Employees Take Charge." *Inc.* (October 1995).

CHAPTER 5

Screening Candidates

INTRODUCTION

The success of any recruiting effort, as pointed out in the previous chapter, is ultimately measured by the number of qualified candidates it produces. But a good response to a recruiting effort can be a mixed blessing. True, it enhances the chances of ending up with an outstanding employee, but it also creates pressures for the people who must process the resumes, handle the letters and calls, and whittle down the list of applicants to a manageable number.

In the past, an overabundance of applicants wasn't a major problem for many large companies, thanks to the presence of large and well-staffed human resources departments. And when it comes to attracting candidates in certain high-skill areas, the problem today is rarely a surplus of responses, but a shortfall.

But regardless of the number of qualified responses, the responsibility of screening candidates has been increasingly assumed by either business owners or line managers who cannot afford to spend the time necessary to narrow a large field of applicants down to a short list of genuine candidates. This chapter looks at how progressive companies are handling this new challenge.

SCREENING NEEDS TO BE LOGICAL AND COORDINATED

The key to an effective screening process is recognizing, first of all, what the process is meant to accomplish. Screening, especially in the early stages, is not meant to determine which candidate is the "best." Its purpose instead is to narrow down the field of likely candidates so that the bulk of time and effort can be directed toward those candidates who deserve the most attention. Companies that have an excellent record of hiring effectively generally view screening as a "whittling process," the idea being to narrow the field in a logical, multistage manner, with the criteria for staying in contention rising as the process moves along. In some of these companies, the recruiting process has been likened to the "rushing" rites of an exclusive fraternity or sorority or, better still, the tryout regimen for would-be astronauts. The company, in other words, considers it a given that only a small percentage of the people who are initially contacted in the earliest stages of recruiting will be around once the hiring process has been completed.

In these instances, the resume is typically not the principal screening device. Candidates are generally screened via a brief phone interview, which becomes the first obstacle in the process. Candidates who pass the phone screening are then invited to the company's offices for face-to-face interviews. Also typically, the interview process consists of several stages, with differing criteria in each stage. Early on, for instance, interviewers might be looking for one quality, such as enthusiasm or interest in the company's products. Candidates that come across very strongly in this phase of the process move on to the next stage, during which they might be asked, for example, to role-play a sales call.

In some instances, candidates who do well in the second phase of the process move on to a more intensive level of interviewing, which may involve additional role-playing exercises as well as receiving a more in-depth presentation about the culture, products, and technology of the company.

Candidates who pass this stage successfully are often offered a position with the company.

On the surface, the steps in this screening process may seem unduly cumbersome. The theory today, however, is that the effort it takes to screen candidates in a disciplined, rigorous manner more than pays for itself in the future, sparing the company the time and expense associated with hiring mistakes.

SELF-DEFENSE: A CRASH COURSE IN EMPLOYMENT LAW

Many people are under the false—and dangerous—assumption that it is only during the actual interviewing process that companies run the risk of violating the state and federal laws that prohibit discriminatory practices in hiring. Not so. Virtually everything that happens during the hiring process—particularly during the screening phase of the process—has implications that could conceivably lead to lawsuits. People involved in screening don't need to be employment law "experts," but they should at least be aware of the most important of these laws and what they are designed to do.

1. *The Civil Rights Act of 1964:* Forbids arbitrary, artificial, and unnecessary barriers to employment based on the race, sex, national origin, ancestry, or religious beliefs of the candidate.
2. *The Pregnancy Discrimination Act of 1978:* Prohibits job discrimination on the basis of pregnancy or related medical conditions.
3. *The Age Discrimination in Employment Act (as amended in 1978):* Prohibits discrimination in hiring of individuals age 40 and older.
4. *The Americans with Disabilities Act of 1990:* Prohibits discrimination against physically and mentally disabled individuals whose disabilities are not directly connected to job performance.
5. *The Fair Labor Standards Act, as amended by the Equal Pay Act:* Sets minimum wages, as well as overtime and equal pay standards.
6. *The Immigration Reform and Control Act of 1986:* Prohibits the employment of illegal

Stellar Performer
Prescreening, Southwest Airlines Style

Dallas, Texas-based Southwest Airlines is known throughout the airline industry for its unusually low turnover rate and for the extraordinarily high morale of its workforce. The company's reputation as a great place to work is so strong, in fact, that each year it receives more than 150,000 applications, of which only a fraction (4,500) are hired.

How does the company that attracts so many applicants handle screening? According to a report in *Fast Company* magazine, with depth, imagination, and intensity. Applicants for flight attendants positions, for example, must first attend a large open-house-type meeting, usually held in a hotel conference room. The purpose of that first meeting is to give Southwest Airlines an idea early on of whether the applicant has "the perfect blend of energy, humor, team spirit, and self-confidence to match Southwest's customer-obsessed culture." Instead of a typical application, candidates fill out a questionnaire that contains such statements as:

- "One time my sense of humor helped me was . . ."
- "My personal motto is . . ."
- "One time I reached my peak performance was . . ."

Southwest Airlines has also created what its human resources executives consider a highly reliable way to gain insight into the leadership skills of applicants. It is a group exercise called "Fallout Shelters." Applicants are broken into groups and instructed to imagine that they're members of a committee whose job is to rebuild civilization in light of a just-declared nuclear war. They are then given a list of 15 people from different occupations, including nurse, teacher, and professional athlete, and are told that just six can remain in the only available fallout shelter (and presumably be the basis for the team that will rebuild the world). As the groups debate the issue, recruiters move throughout the room taking note of those who are contributing the most to the discussion. After the session, recruiters meet, compare notes, and call back a small number of the most promising for in-depth interviews.[1]

aliens (applies to all hires, with no exceptions for small companies or household employment). Prohibits discrimination against qualified applicants based on national origin or citizenship status.

7. *The Uniformed Services Employment and Reemployment Act of 1994:* Prohibits discrimination based on uniformed service.

It behooves every company to make sure that anyone involved with the hiring process is aware of at least the basic principles of each of these laws, as well of whatever state statutes might apply regarding hiring practices. A good place to get detailed information about employment law is the EEOC (Equal Employment Opportunity Commission) Web site at http://www.gsa.gov/eeo per KR). Given the complexities of employment law today, however, companies would be well advised to review their current employment policies with an employment law specialist (see Table 5.1). In-house attorneys are the most logical option for companies that are large enough to afford their own legal staffs. Otherwise, the task is best handled by outside counsel whose expertise is not limited solely to EEOC regulations but encompasses state and local regulations as well.

KEY CONCEPT

SCREENING RESUMES

The most common method of narrowing down the field of applicants for any given job is to sort through resumes. The main advantage of this effort is efficiency: A resume can be reviewed in a moment or two and criteria can be set up that make it fairly easy to start eliminating. There are, however, numerous drawbacks to resume sorting as a screening device, such as those that follow.

- Resume sorting can be an exceptionally tedious task, especially when there are hundreds of resumes for the same position.
- Resume screening as the main method of narrowing the field of candidates favors people who are skilled at writing resumes but who may not be the best candidates.

TABLE 5.1 PLAYING IT SAFE

Laws designed to prevent discrimination can be bewildering to anyone who does not specialize in employment law, but there's an easy enough way to avoid trouble. To stay on the safe side, recruiting practices should always be keyed to bona fide qualifications. It is unwise to discuss any aspect of recruiting—including the questions asked during prescreening or on the application—that touches on the following areas.

- Age
- Appearance (height and weight)
- Arrest and criminal records (except those that might have a direct impact on the position to be filled)
- Financial status
- Marital status
- Number of children
- Proficiency in English
- National origin
- Religion

As stated above, it is safest to consult with legal counsel.

- Sorting criteria are sometimes arbitrary, eliminating candidates who should be given a closer look.

But probably the biggest drawback to basing candidate screening solely on information found in resumes is that resumes are notoriously unreliable when it comes to revealing the intangible qualities that have become increasingly important in most jobs today. When Nordstrom, for instance, is hiring retail clerks for its department stores, it places more importance on a candidate's "friendliness" than on that person's "merchandising experience."[2] And more and more these days, the people who work in manufacturing facilities need to be able to bring to the job communication skills and other personal traits that lend themselves to the newer, team-based cultures.

It is possible to infer these qualities by reading between the lines of a resume (see Table 5.2). One can reasonably assume, for instance, that a candidate who belongs to a variety of organizations enjoys working with groups. Similarly, it could be assumed that candidates who have excelled at team sports in either high school or college might

TABLE 5.2 READING BETWEEN THE LINES

As long as the person who is screening resumes recognizes that analyzing them is neither pure art nor pure science, the process yields some reasonable, productive information. Here are the key categories of information that resumes may contain, along with some questions worth asking when absorbing the information.

Personal data. Some applicants, either intentionally or unintentionally, include personal data, such as their age, sex, marital status, number of children, height, and weight. This kind of information should be disregarded. Personal data should not be considered in the hiring process. The candidate may not realize the information is irrelevant or that it's illegal for an interviewer to discuss any of the above during the interview.

Career objective. Key question: How closely does the job objective section of the resume (if there is such a section) match the particulars of the job being filled? Key concern: Savvy applicants will generally tailor the job objective section to the specific position that needs to be filled. Consequently, a match between the job objective as written and the job itself should be taken with a grain of salt. But when the objective on the resume is clearly at odds with the nature of the job at hand, the candidate should be given low priority. Either the job seeker didn't take the time to read the ad, or he or she is simply applying for every job opening encountered.

Previous employers. How closely did the values and cultures of those companies (as far as anyone knows) match the values and culture of your firm?

Tasks performed. What specific accomplishments can be inferred from the description of duties and responsibilities handled in prior jobs? How instrumental, in short, was the candidate in developing new ideas, bringing in business, solving problems?

Education. It is hard *not* to be influenced one way or the other by the reputation of the college or university the candidate attended. Certain schools do indeed have much higher admission standards than others, which may mean this variable could be a reasonably accurate indicator of the candidate's general intelligence. The majority of CEOs in the United States today, however, did not attend Ivy League colleges.

be better suited to team-oriented cultures than candidates who have excelled at individual sports such as track or tennis.

Keep in mind, though, that these are only assumptions. The fact remains that it is extremely difficult to determine with any degree of certainty what a candidate is really like on the basis of the resume and cover letter. Compounding this problem is the fact that more and more resumes today have been professionally prepared, specifically designed to create a winning impression, never mind that the impression may not provide an accurate picture of who the candidate is.

The implications? Managers and business owners who rely on resumes as the primary means of narrowing the field need to recognize the limitations of this approach. If they screen solely on the basis of this most obvious criterion, they run the risk of ending up with a list of finalists whose chief strength is their ability to write resumes that can survive the screening process.

KEY CONCEPT

BE SYSTEMATIC

Resume screening should be handled in a disciplined manner, with the criteria used for screening clearly spelled out.

How the screening process is actually handled will depend, in most cases, on how many resumes are involved and who (or, in the case of resume scanners and database software, what) is responsible for deciding which candidates deserve a closer look and which don't. Companies that process an unusually high volume of resumes for the same job have one of two options. One is to delegate a good part of the responsibility for screening to somebody other than the line manager who will be doing the actual hiring. The other is to rely on technology.

Several new technological options for resume screening have come to the fore in recent years. Some companies today use optical scanners to convert the information printed on the resume into computer data that can be stored and sorted in a database. The database can then be programmed to select candidates on the basis of key words that can single out resumes from candidates that have a specific kind of work background. Advocates of these programs emphasize their efficiency: the fact that scanners can accomplish in a matter of hours what might otherwise take days or weeks. Skeptics point out that the most sophisticated of these resume-sorting programs—especially those that are customized to a company's specific needs—can be expensive: The price tag, including hardware and training, can run into the hundreds of thousands of dollars. It's been argued, too, that the state of the art in many of these programs still leaves much to be desired. Many scanners, for instance, can't convert resumes that are written in unusual typefaces. And the search functions in the new software can't begin to take into account the many varieties of work experiences that might be embodied in any of the terms or words used as a narrowing device.

JOB CANDIDATES CAN FOOL THE SCANNERS

Job seekers have become wise to the practice of incorporating buzzwords or industry-specific terms in their resumes in order to appear more attractive to employers who use software to screen for key words. Don't become overly reliant on this software and be sure to ask enough in-depth questions during the telephone screening to verify key skill areas.

DON'T BE "CREDENTIAL BLIND"

Before any group of resumes is reviewed, the person doing the screening must have a clear idea of what specific factors will be used as the main screening criteria. Make sure that the factors that differentiate strong candidates from the "definitely nots" are genuinely valid indicators of job performance. Noted author and speaker Tom Peters, for example, has long warned companies not to become too preoccupied with credentials as a screening factor. American companies, he maintains, tend to overemphasize not only the MBA ("to a disgraceful degree") but technical diplomas as well. To prove the folly of this practice, Peters has cited on many occasions the case of Honda Motor Co., Inc., which, he says, is "responsible for a disproportionate share of automotive technical breakthroughs and yet has only three Ph.D.s on its engineering staff."[3]

When looking over a resume, try to find signs that the candidate recognizes that businesses are run to make a profit. Key sign: Do important results and accomplishments listed on the resume show a recognition of the importance of the bottom line?

USE QUALITY CONTROL FOR SCREENING PROCESSES

To make sure that the screening process a company has developed isn't inadvertently eliminating from consideration candidates who should be interviewed, choose a random handful of resumes from the "reject" pile and call those who are most qualified. If, after a brief phone conversation, it turns out that those candidates deserve more scrutiny, the criteria used for screening should be reexamined or the system itself should be retooled.

TWO RESUME FORMATS AND WHAT TO LOOK FOR IN EACH

A typical stack of resumes usually contains two distinct types: (1) *chronological,* in which information is organized from year to year in a more or less sequential manner, with job responsibilities described on a position-by-position basis; and (2) *functional,* in which information is organized according to skills or general work experience.

Large corporations have traditionally preferred chronological resumes because they are easier to read and can provide a more accurate picture of a candidate's work experience and progression. But as more and more candidates these days are applying for jobs that do not represent the next logical step in a career path, the proportion of functional resumes is on the rise.

Here are some considerations to bear in mind when reviewing each type of resume (see Table 5.3).

Chronological

- *Length of employment:* When listing dates of employment, did the applicant include at least the month and year the work experience began and ended? (Remember, "1991" could mean anywhere from one week to 12 months.)
- *Gaps:* Are employment dates in sequence, or is there a gap? Is the gap explained elsewhere in the resume (perhaps the applicant was in school)? If not, what was he or she doing?

TABLE 5.3 RESUME RED FLAGS: HOW TO WEED OUT THE WEAKEST CANDIDATES

It's impossible to know for certain whether the way a resume is written accurately mirrors the skills and qualifications of the candidate, but here are four of the most common characteristics found on the resumes of candidates who may have something to hide.

- *Functional resume that has no dates and doesn't list companies.* Could mean candidate has significant gaps in employment.
- *An excess of information about hobbies and interests.* Could indicate an unwillingness to work extra hours.
- *An excess of detailed information about courses, educational honors, and club memberships.* The key here is how relevant that information is to the job at hand.
- *An excess of qualifiers and hedgers.* Phrases such as "exposure to" and "familiar with" usually indicate that the candidate lacks hands-on experience.

- *Longevity:* How long, in general, has the candidate worked at jobs? Too many jobs in too short a time could be the red flag, indicating that the candidate may have trouble adjusting to different work environments.

Functional

- *Lack of specifics:* Candidates who only mention their "skills" in their resumes and have very little to say about the specific companies they've worked for are probably doing so intentionally and would rather their previous work experience not be a factor in the selection process.
- *Evidence of accomplishment:* If a candidate can make a strong case for the skills and traits described in a functional resume, previous work experience may not be as important, and the candidate probably deserves a closer look.

Tip

HOW THE PROS SCREEN RESUMES

Recruiters who specialize in finding candidates for jobs in which the number of applicants vastly exceeds the number of positions have been forced, by the nature of the task, to develop their own screening criteria. Here's a brief look at what the pros consider when they're deciding whether a resume should be put in the "active" file or the "other" file.

- *Overall appearance of the resume:* How neat and professional-looking it is. (A superficial criterion, true, but it could be important in certain types of jobs in which making a good impression is important.)
- *Career growth pattern:* Whether the sequence of jobs the candidate has held reveals a discernible pattern of increasing responsibility and accomplishment.
- *Depth of work descriptions:* How detailed the candidate has been in describing the specific duties and responsibilities of jobs listed on the resume, and whether the description reveals an awareness of what's important and what isn't.
- *The quality of the writing:* A resume isn't meant to be a work of literary art, but resumes filled with typos, misspellings, and grammatical mistakes do not speak well for the candidate's ability to pay attention to detail (see Table 5.4).

TABLE 5.4 COMIC RELIEF: RESUME GAFFES

Here are some excerpts from "*Resumania,*" a term coined by Robert Half, founder of Robert Half International, for his collection of inadvertent mistakes, typos, and inappropriate information from various job candidates' resumes, applications, and cover letters. Half's "*Resumania*" appears in his monthly column in *National Business Employment Weekly.* He constantly receives new submissions for his collection. The following are some recent examples, along with Half's commentary.

- "Excellant at people oriented positi9ons and organiztional problem solving." (But not so good at proofreading.)
- "I am a great team player I am." (And I do not like green eggs and ham!)
- "I have lurnt Word Perfect 6.0, computor and spreadsheat progroms." (But has yet to master the spell check.)
- "Very experienced with out-house computers." (Where did they find an extension cord that long?)
- "1881–1995: Spent my time teaching and going to school for computer science." (That's all in 114 years?)
- "To Home-Ever it concerns." (We'll forward it right away.)
- "Received a plague for Salesperson of the Year." (Get well soon!)

Stellar Performers

Here is what the chief executives from three rapidly growing companies say about screening candidates.

The unicycle factor. "When I am looking to hire producers," says Steve Rosenbaum, president of Broadcast News Networks, "I look for information in the resume that reflects spirit and energy." Example: One of the producers Rosenbaum hired indicated in his resume that he had "unicycled across the United States." Explains Rosenbaum: "I was impressed that the guy had gone out on a limb and put that bit of information in a resume."

The best offense. Kathy Ericksen, chief executive officer of CAPSCO of Sunnyvale, California, asks the same eight questions to each candidate she screens by phone. Every one of the questions, she says, is "characterological": It sheds light on the candidate as a person. Examples include: "Who do you consider to be the most successful person you've ever known?" and "In the past, have you been criticized for your work, and if so, how did you respond?" The point of the second question, says Ms. Ericksen, is to weed out "defensive" candidates.

Foul play. While screening candidates for his information technology company, David Blumenthal, president of Flash Creative Management, likes to ask probing questions about specific aspects of a candidate's resume. On one occasion, Blumenthal noticed that the candidate had noted on his resume that he'd been a member of the university's all-league basketball team. Blumenthal brought up the point during the first screening interview. He wanted to know about the candidate's free-throw shooting average, and was happy to discover that it was 95 percent. His reasoning? "The only way you can really excel at foul shots," explains Blumenthal, "is to practice." Explained Blumenthal, "A 95 percent rate demonstrates to us that the applicant had a commitment to being the best."[4]

For more pointers on phone screening, see Table 5.5.

TABLE 5.5 HOW TO SCREEN EFFECTIVELY BY PHONE

Interviewing techniques in general are covered in depth in Chapter 6. In the meantime, though, here are some specific guidelines on how to use a phone conversation as an effective screening device.

- Set an agenda for the phone call, based on the amount of time needed to screen by phone all candidates that need to be contacted.
- Ask all candidates the same general mix of questions for a common basis of comparison.
- If a candidate seems very promising, cut the phone conversation short and set up a face-to-face interview.
- If the applicant isn't available and it's necessary to leave a call-back message, set a time for the callback the next day. It's a little thing, but candidates who fail to return the call at the designated time or don't call back earlier to explain why they can't do so could be demonstrating one of two things: (1) a lack of interest in the job; or (2) a lack of discipline and commitment.
- Always have a copy of the applicant's resume and cover letter when making the phone call.
- Begin the conversation by telling the candidate that this is a preliminary interview and by giving a brief outline of the job duties.
- Spell out the tasks and responsibilities of the job, rather than the skills and qualities being sought.
- Address any questions that have arisen during the review of the candidate's resume.
- Ask candidates directly what they believe they can bring to the job.
- Unless there's a desperate need, don't try to "oversell" the job to the applicant.

- *The cover letter:* Recruiting pros like to see letters that indicate the author's familiarity with the company. If nothing else, it demonstrates that the candidate understands the competitive nature of job hunting and takes a proactive approach to challenges.

DON'T SCREEN OUT ARBITRARILY

DANGER!

Factors used to eliminate candidates from further consideration should always be directly related to the success criteria of the job. The fact that a resume isn't written particularly well, for instance, would be a good reason to eliminate from contention someone who has

Stellar Performer: Gnossos Software Getting It in Writing

One way to narrow the field for any job opening that draws an unusually large response is to follow the example of Steve Kantor, president of Gnossos Software in Washington, DC. Kantor's strategy is to select the top 20 percent of applicants—based on their resumes—and to send each a "congratulations-on-being-selected-for-consideration" letter in which he or she is asked to answer the following questions in another letter.

- What are your greatest strengths?
- What are your weaknesses?

Occasionally, too, Kantor will throw in an off-the-wall question on an unrelated topic. (Kantor says he is usually "half kidding" with these questions, but is curious to see what kind of a response the question elicits.) He's impressed when candidates want to know what that question has to do with being an effective employee.

Kantor's reasoning is as follows: Only those candidates who have strong drive and ambition will be motivated to go to the next step in the process. Kantor reviews every letter himself and then interviews the top candidates by phone. He deliberately holds off on face-to-face interviews, he says, because he doesn't want to be unduly influenced by the candidate's appearance.[5]

to communicate in writing. But it might not be a valid screening factor for a telemarketer, for example.

APPLICATION FORMS: KEEP IT SIMPLE

Application forms in most companies are a lot simpler and more streamlined today than they used to be (see Table 5.6), mainly because of the many questions (about age, gender, or marital status, for instance) that are now considered discriminatory. Many companies today don't even bother with standard application forms, relying instead on the candidate's resume.

PHYSICAL EXAMINATIONS

Companies are permitted to ask employees to undergo a physical examination as a condition of employment—but only after a job offer has been extended. Companies that require physical examinations as a condition of employment should consult legal counsel to make sure that whatever "physical requirements" the company has established fall within the guidelines set by the Rehabilitation Act of 1973, the Americans with Disabilities Act of 1990, or similar state laws, and that the procedures followed in administering the exams and reviewing the results comply with all legal requirements, including protecting the candidate's right of privacy.

TABLE 5.6 BASICS OF AN APPLICATION FORM

- Name, address, telephone number, and so on
- Educational level: names and cities of high school and college attended; degrees earned
- Prior work experience from at least three previous employers, including name of company and supervisor, and job description
- Special licenses or awards
- References

Stellar Performer: **Gates Rubber Cutting Turnover at a Rubber Plant**

According to a 1994 article in *Inc.* magazine, when Gates Rubber, in Solam, Arkansas, analyzed its business operations several years ago, senior management went beyond the typical line-item analysis and began to factor into its bottom line such hiring-related factors as the cost of quality mistakes, injuries, and work slowdowns as a result of overtime costs. The result: The company found that hiring mistakes constituted its number one expense.

The task of revitalizing the process fell to the company's plant manager, who responded by creating a multiphase process built around the notion of eliminating those applicants who may look promising on the surface but won't be able to meet the actual requirements of the job. Here are the key elements of the process.

Phase one. A general interview with the human resources department, which does the preliminary screening based on education, experience, and the general impression created at the interview.

Phase two. A second interview with someone else from human resources to verify information and impressions from the first meeting.

Phase three. A panel interview with three people (including the plant manager) from different parts of the plant, during which time the candidate is evaluated on the basis of communications skills, work attitude, and general confidence level. Since all the work in the plant is done in teams, the company focuses on a candidate's ability to respond well in a group setting. The results speak for themselves. Gates' annual turnover is roughly 8 percent, compared to 100 percent turnover at a comparable plant owned by another company in town.[6]

END POINT

Screening job candidates is by no means a science, but companies with successful hiring practices almost invariably have systematic screening procedures in place. Care must be taken to ensure that screening criteria are based on bona fide qualifications; otherwise a company could unwittingly open itself up to charges of discrimination. Procedures need to be reasonably flexible as well. An overly structured approach to resume screening, for instance, can often work to the disadvantage of candidates who may lack certain credentials but possess intangible attributes—such as resourcefulness or flexibility—that can make the difference between good employees and outstanding ones. Chief among the pitfalls to be avoided in this respect is "credential blindness"—building screening criteria arbitrarily around degrees earned and colleges attended instead of the candidate's overall abilities.

The actual process of screening should follow a logical pattern. A careful review of a resume will usually separate those candidates who are grossly misrepresenting themselves from those whose resume data can be taken at face value. But it's generally a good practice to hold brief telephone conversations with as many candidate prospects as practically possible before granting face-to-face interviews.

MORE READING

Carbonara, Peter. "Best Practices: Hiring." *Inc.* (March 1994).

———. "Fire Me. I Dare You!" *Inc.* (March 1997).

Commentary, "Welfare Reform: Tougher Times Ahead." *Business Week* (May 5, 1997).

"Hiring Through Resume Databases." *Inc.* (May 1993).

Mamis, Robert A. "Employees from Hell." *Inc.* (January 1995).

Mcgovern, Marion. "Behind the Times." *Inc.* (October 1995).

Nelson, Bob. *1001 Ways to Reward Employees.* New York: Workman Publishing, 1994.

Posner, Bruce G. "Hiring the Best." *Inc.* (April 1989).

Quintanilla, Carl. "As Jobs Go Begging, Bosses Toil Nights—and Improvise." *The Wall Street Journal.* (March 1997).

Stidger, Ruth W. *The Competence Game: How to Find, Use, and Keep Competent Employees.* New York: Thomond Press, 1980.

Yate, Martin John. *Hiring the Best.* Boston, Massachusetts: Peregrine McCoy, Ltd., 1987.

CHAPTER 6

The Art of Effective Interviewing

INTRODUCTION

The employment interview, sometimes known as the "selection" or "evaluation" interview, is almost universally regarded as the single most important aspect of the hiring process. But while everybody agrees that at some point in the hiring process there needs to be at least one face-to-face meeting (preferably several) between the candidate and the hiring manager, there is considerable debate about how interviews should be conducted. And there are widely differing views on whether a candidate's performance during an interview is a valid predictor of actual work performance. Numerous studies have been conducted to shed light on this critical question, but the results have been inconclusive—and for the most obvious of reasons: There are simply too many variables that might affect the correlation.

This debate notwithstanding, when handled properly, a face-to-face interview can yield information about a candidate that no other screening or assessment mechanism can.

But when the job interview is mishandled—that is, approached in an undisciplined, haphazard way and conducted by individuals who neither understand nor respect the dynamics of the process—this valuable "tool" can suddenly become a minefield. Indeed, the vast majority of hiring mistakes can be traced to a hiring process that relies too much on the "gut" judgments of managers who base their hiring decisions almost solely on assessments they make during the interview.

This chapter provides a detailed look at the art of interviewing—in particular, at those skills that underlie the ability to handle this critical aspect of hiring efficiently and intelligently.

KEY CONCEPT

WHAT THE "SCIENCE" SHOWS

The issue of interviews being accurate performance indicators has been studied extensively over the past 40 years, but with mixed results. The main problem lies with methodology. It is virtually impossible to design a study that can take into account all the variables that can affect the correlation between interview-based evaluations and job performance. These variables include the following.

- The validity of the hiring criteria
- The level of genuine interest the applicant had in the job and how diligently he or she prepared for the interview
- The skill of the interviewer in handling the interview process in general
- The actual conditions of the interview—where it took place, how long it took, whether there were interruptions, and so on
- The nature of the job (whether anything changed—a new supervisor, for instance—between the time the interview was held and the time the employee actually began work)
- The extent to which the interviewer was willing to probe when the answers were incomplete
- The interviewer's listening skills

These variables notwithstanding, studies on the selection interview allow us to make the following generalizations about the process itself and what can reasonably be expected from it.

- Whatever its limitations, the interview (when conducted properly and by people who understand the process) is the most important element in the hiring process.
- The ability of a candidate to create a good impression during an interview is a skill unto itself, and the qualities that underlie that skill do not necessarily match the qualities that underlie effective performance on the job.
- There is a direct correlation between the skill and experience of the interviewer and the general reliability of the assessments that interviewers make on the candidate's suitability for hiring.

THE CHANGING ROLE OF THE JOB INTERVIEW

Job interviews in progressive companies are viewed much differently than they used to be. The interview is still the primary assessment tool, but companies with successful hiring practices are no longer as willing as they once were to base hiring decisions on a single interview—particularly when conducted by somebody who has little experience in the process.

One company well known for the depth of its interviewing process is Hewlett-Packard, where candidates go through as many as a half-dozen interviews—often with different people throughout the organization. There are definite risks to this committee-like approach to hiring. The primary risk is that the final choice will not be the "best" choice but rather the candidate that the majority of the interviewers find least objectionable. Nevertheless, Hewlett-Packard uses multiple interviews to not only bring more voices into the process but to, in effect, inundate the candidate with the company's values. That way, if the candidate is ultimately hired, the orientation will have long since been under way and the candidate will already be acclimated to the company's culture. Tom Peters has described Hewlett-Packard's hiring process as a "lengthy courtship." "HP lives its values so openly," he once noted, "that if a person is going to be uncomfortable in the company, the discomfort will start during the interviewing process and candidates that don't fit in will generally leave of their own accord."[1]

As consultant Gregory Lousig-Nont told *USA Today Magazine* in 1996, "The days of filling out a standard application form and hiring on a 'gut feeling' are gone."[2]

THE UNWRITTEN RULES OF THE GAME

The dynamics of a typical job interview have often been compared to a "chess game" of sorts, with both principals—the applicant and the interviewer—doing their utmost to outthink and outfox each other.

Ideally, the job interview would be a frank conversation between two people in which the interviewer would spell out, right from the start, the criteria he or she was using to judge candidates. The candidate would make an objective and accurate self-assessment of whether he or she met those criteria. But because the objectives of the job candidate and interviewer are not necessarily in sync, what happens in reality is much different.

The main agenda of the person being interviewed, obviously, is to make a favorable impression, to convince the interviewer that he or she possesses whatever the interviewer is looking for in a winning candidate. Interviewees who bring this mind-set into the interview room are not necessarily being deceptive. In most cases, they genuinely believe that, given a chance, they can be good at the job for which they are applying. And if they're savvy (or have been coached and groomed in job-interviewing techniques), they're going to be doing their best to showcase their strengths and conceal their weaknesses.

When *USA Today* talked to executives in December 1996 about the way the hiring game is being played throughout the United States, it found the field to be more skewed in favor of the candidates. "Very few job candidates are so naive as to attempt to 'wing it' in an interview," the newspaper reported. "Moreover, there are those applicants—namely job-hoppers and sociopaths—who have an almost uncanny ability to tell interviewers exactly what they want to hear."[3]

But interviewers have their own set of objectives, too. Because it is becoming tougher and tougher to get reliable reference information, interviewers today face an unusually difficult challenge. As often as not, the questions that have always been the bedrock of the job interview—"Tell me about yourself," "What did you like (or dislike) about your last job?"—produce answers that candidates have carefully prepared in advance to make the most favorable impression.

In reality, hiring managers would much rather hear a truthful answer than the "right" answer.

In a survey developed and conducted by Robert Half International in 1996, executives were asked, "Other than the ability and willingness to do the job, what is the one quality that impresses you the most about a candidate during a job interview?" Thirty-two percent of the survey respondents cited honesty and integrity as the most impressive quality. In a similar survey conducted in 1991, this attribute was listed last (receiving 7 percent of the votes).

Many of the seemingly straightforward questions that savvy interviewers ask are intended to do more than simply generate information—they are also crafted to get the candidate to reveal personality traits that he or she may wish to conceal.

How does an interviewer become more proficient at this "game?" In two ways: first, by understanding the dynamics (and the limitations) of the interview process; and second, by developing the skills and, more importantly, the discipline required to maximize the process.

KEY CONCEPT

PREPARATION MATTERS

One of the main causes of interview assessments that ultimately lead to hiring "mistakes" also happens to be one of the easiest to correct. It has to do with preparation—taking sufficient time *before* the interview to think through the process, clarify objectives, and prepare for the interview itself. The interviewer must prepare mentally, by reviewing the candidate's application materials, and physically, by creating an appropriately quiet and undisturbed interview space. See Table 6.1 for a pre-interview preparation checklist.

"Managers who consistently interview poorly," says Bob Bogart, executive vice president of human resources for Mutual of Omaha, "almost invariably underestimate both the importance and the difficulty of the process. Instead of treating the interview with any sense of urgency, they 'wing' it. So right from the start, they reduce the chances of getting information that is truly useful when the time comes to assess an individual candidate or compare a group of candidates."

The most important element in the preparation process, by far, is making sure that the questions that will be asked during the interview are

TABLE 6.1 A PRE-INTERVIEW CHECKLIST: SEVEN TASKS THAT INTERVIEWERS SHOULD COMPLETE *BEFORE* THE INTERVIEW

1. Formulate a set of hiring criteria that accurately reflect the demands of the job.
2. Thoroughly familiarize themselves with those criteria and develop a set of questions expressly designed to yield information directly related to the criteria.
3. Review the candidate's resume and cover letter and make note of areas that need clarification or elaboration.
4. Determine the objective of the interview (i.e., to screen candidates or to determine which finalist is the best choice).
5. Develop a general plan for the interview that allots sufficient time for each of the areas of the candidate's background or personality that need to be explored.
6. Schedule the interview for a time when the interviewers can focus on the task at hand.
7. Take reasonable measures (holding calls, closing the door, etc.) to make sure that there are no distractions.

directly related to clearly defined hiring criteria, including the specific skills or personal attributes required. "What happens when you *don't* have a very clear idea of what combination of skills and traits the job requires," Bogart says, "is that managers tend to be swayed by personal factors that have little bearing on a candidate's ability to do the job. And by doing so, they play right into the hands of those candidates whose main qualification is that they know how to handle themselves well in the interview."[4]

MAKE SURE THE INTERVIEW HAS AN EFFICIENT STRUCTURE

A typical selection interview only lasts for one or two hours. To make the most efficient use of this time, good interviewers usually map out the agenda ahead of time, making a list of the areas they want to cover and the questions they want to ask. Part of this process involves setting priorities—differentiating those questions that are directly related to the fundamental hiring criteria from those that are tangentially related—and preparing a general timeline that allots an appropriate amount of time for each issue.

KEEP SMALL TALK TO A MINIMUM

A certain amount of time is generally set aside for greeting the candidate and for small talk designed to put the candidate at ease. Generally, though, the "small talk" part of the interview is best kept to a minimum. Other suggestions to make the interview more productive include the following.

- Do whatever is reasonably possible to make the candidate feel welcome and relaxed.
- Begin the "formal" part of the interview (after the greeting) with an overview of what the meeting is meant to accomplish and how long it will take.
- Ask questions slowly and make sure the candidate understands exactly what he or she is being asked.

- Be sensitive to the pressures the candidate is feeling but don't allow that sensitivity to prevent the asking of substantive, probing questions.
- Try not to rush things, even though there might be other issues pressing.
- Try to follow the "agenda" as closely as possible, allowing sufficient time for all the key issues to be addressed.
- Leave adequate time for questions from the candidate.
- If the candidate seems promising and time is running out, schedule another interview.

GETTING BETTER AT THE ART

A critical skill in the art of interviewing is the ability to interact with people in a way that puts them at ease. Being able to do so enhances the likelihood that people will communicate openly and honestly (even when it comes to revealing information they might normally be reluctant to share). See Table 6.2 for an overview of questioning techniques.

People who are naturally gregarious, who enjoy conversation, and who are by nature curious about what makes other people tick are usually better at conducting job interviews than people who are by nature introverted—providing, of course, they're able put that inclination to strategic use. The key is *involvement*—being genuinely interested in what people have to say. Highly successful television interviewers—Barbara Walters and Larry King, for instance—have said repeatedly that the main reason for their success as interviewers stems from the fact that they truly enjoy getting other people to talk about themselves. So when they respond to a comment by asking, "Really?" or "Is that right?" they're not simply going through the motions. They are genuinely surprised, and the people they're interviewing are all the more responsive because of it.

But beyond the ability to get people to communicate openly, interviewers need to be reasonably tough-minded, assertive, and well focused (see

TABLE 6.2 GETTING A HANDLE ON QUESTIONING TECHNIQUES

Another component of skillful interviewing involves the ability to vary questioning techniques according to the personality of the candidate and the conditions that are unique to a specific interview. As most people know, these questioning techniques can be divided into the following types.

- *Closed.* Questions that call for a single-word answer (often yes or no). Examples: "How many people did you supervise in your last job? Did you enjoy working on so many projects at one time?" Closed questions should be used in two ways: (1) to elicit a piece of specific information that fills a gap; or (2) as a prelude to a second question designed to elicit a more general and reflective response.
- *Open-ended.* Questions (often statements) that invite more elaborate answers, either informational or attitudinal. Examples: "Tell me a little about the department you supervised in your last job." "What was it like managing so many different projects at the same time?" Use these questions throughout the interview, but mix in more narrowly defined questions when the candidate's responses begin to move off the track.
- *Leading.* Questions that either intentionally or inadvertently tip the candidate off as to the "preferred" answer. "You don't mind working on weekends, do you?" or "You've handled large budgets in the past, haven't you?"
- *Hypothetical.* Questions that oblige candidates to imagine how they would react in certain situations. "What would you do if you were asked to manage a number of different projects at the same time—and knew you couldn't accomplish them all?"

Table 6.3). Most important, they need to be willing to probe when a candidate's answer is vague or doesn't go far enough. "There's a very fine line between probing and interrogating," says Jim Bofinger, vice president of human resources of Cirrus Logic, Inc., who has counseled hiring managers in the computer business for more than 15 years. "It has to be done gradually. Regardless of how important a piece of information may be, you can't always elicit it by coming out and asking for it directly. If you do, the person can become defensive. You have to coax the information out a little bit at a time, the way Peter Falk does it in *Columbo.*"[5]

MIRROR FOR CLARIFICATION

As long as it's not overdone, the interviewing technique generally known as *mirror probe* or *restating* is a useful tool for getting candidates to relax

TABLE 6.3 QUESTIONING WISDOM FROM THE PROS

Studies of successful interviewers reveal the following practices:

- *Easy openers.* These people generally begin their interviews with open, "broad-brush" questions—questions that are unthreatening and relatively easy to answer. Rationale: to get the conversation rolling and put the candidate in a relaxed state of mind.
- *Effective tandems.* As the interview progresses, skillful questioners ask questions in tandem: a closed question easily answered, followed by an open question that requires a more thoughtful, more attitude-based response. Example: "What project in your last job did you enjoy working on the most?" followed up with "Tell me why you think that was."
- *Reality, not hypothesis.* They use hypothetical questions sparingly. Rationale: Hypothetical questions encourage candidates to formulate the answers they think the interviewer wants to hear. It's better to couch the question in an actual behavioral context. Instead of, "What would you do if an employee needed to take time off and you and your team were facing a crunching deadline?", try this: "How did you handle things in your last job when an employee came to you and wanted some time off but you and your team were facing a tight deadline crunch?"
- *Going the next step.* They're not afraid to probe. They do it politely but with resolve. And if the candidate doesn't want to answer, they try to find out why.
- *Close to the vest.* Unless they have an excellent reason for doing so, they never precede a question with a statement of their own opinion. Doing so would simply give the candidate an invitation to agree.
- *Quality control.* They don't focus on questions whose answers appear on the application or the resume.

Adapted from: Sam Deep and Lyle Sussman, Smart Moves (Reading, MA: Addison Wesley), 1995, p. 84.

and to be more forthcoming in their answers. The technique consists of following a candidate's answer with a statement that either repeats the answer or expresses the same idea in a slightly different way. Example:

> Candidate: *One of my strengths is that I'm a good team player. I really like the idea of working with others toward the same goal.*
>
> Interviewer: *So you enjoy the team process, good. Can you be a little more specific about what makes you effective when you're a member of a team?*

SEPARATE FACTS FROM IMPRESSIONS WHEN TAKING NOTES

Psychologist John Drake, in *Interviewing for Managers,*[6] advises interviewers to divide the notes they take into two categories: facts and hypotheses. He suggests separating a sheet of paper into two columns. One of the columns, he says, should be used for "facts"—specific information about the candidate's background that isn't found in the resume. The other column should be used for observations that pop into the interviewer's mind in response to something the candidate says or does.

GUARDING AGAINST THE HALO EFFECT

Halo effect is the term commonly used to describe what happens when interviewers become so enamored with—or turned off by—one particular aspect of a candidate that this one particular characteristic, quality, or defect carries a disproportionate amount of weight in the overall assessment. Hence, the interviewer is putting a "halo" on the head of the preferred applicant.

Any number of factors can trigger the halo effect, including educational background (i.e., where the person went to school), interest in a particular subject, proficiency in a sport, and so forth. Whatever the cause, the impact is the same: When the halo effect is working in the positive direction, interviewers invariably overestimate the candidate's other qualities and underestimate the candidate's weaknesses.

If the candidate has the same interests as the interviewer, he or she is seen as the more attractive employee. Candidates who are disorganized are seen as "creative." Candidates who are stubborn are seen as "well-focused." When it is working in a negative direction, the halo effect produces the opposite result. A candidate who attended a rival school may be seen in a negative light. An assertive person is viewed as being "aggressive." Someone who is cordial is seen as "wimpy." Generally, too, the views of an interviewer who is feeling the influence of the halo effect tend to harden as the process moves forward. As social psychologist Eliott Aronson has pointed out, the more a person is committed to a course of action, the more resistant he will be to information that threatens the course.[7]

The main thing to bear in mind about the halo effect is that virtually everyone who conducts an interview is susceptible to it. That susceptibility, moreover, rises when the need is urgent and the supply of qualified candidates is slim. See Table 6.4 for ways to avoid this pitfall.

KEY CONCEPT

DECIDING WHAT TO ASK

The one factor that has more bearing than any other on the reliability of the judgments that emerge from the employment interview has less to do with how the interview is conducted and more to do with the substance of the interview—the questions that are asked. What happens far too often in "cookie-cutter" situations is that the questions being asked today are no different from those asked 40 years ago, and no one knows this better than the experienced job seeker. In most books on job hunting today, job seekers not only are given a glimpse of the questions that "inter-

TABLE 6.4 THREE WAYS INTERVIEWERS CAN MINIMIZE THE IMPACT OF THE HALO EFFECT

There is no single step that an interviewer can take to avoid the skewed judgments that the halo effect can produce. But here are three tips on keeping the tendency under control.

- Study past hiring decisions (particularly the mistakes) and reexamine the principal factors that were given the most weight. If one factor (appearance, for instance) keeps cropping up, chances are it's a factor that is producing the effect.
- Be constantly aware of the tendency to weigh certain factors more heavily than others and make a strong, conscious effort to overcome it.
- Go through an exercise in which the assumption is that the candidate *doesn't* have the one particular quality that is producing the halo effect. How attractive would that candidate be in that situation?

viewers like to ask," but are given detailed instructions on how to answer them.

There is nothing an interviewer can do about the fact that many job seekers today come to the interview well prepared to provide impressive answers to the most commonly asked questions. But the one thing interviewers can do is stick to their own game plans. Except for routine questions designed to put the candidate in a relaxed state of mind, all the questions that are asked during a job interview and all the issues raised should be directly keyed to the hiring criteria.

Creating questions that meet this standard isn't easy by any means, and companies becoming more rigorous in their interviewing practices have typically invested a great deal of time and money developing such questions. What normally happens in these companies is that a group of people recruited from either inside or outside the company takes several months to identify the competencies of the company—those practices and behaviors that distinguish the top performers from the average performers. These competencies are then given behavioral analogues—actions that exemplify the competency—and the combination of competencies and analogues becomes the basis of the hiring criteria and of the questions that are typically asked during the interview.

One example of a company strongly committed to this practice is the Indianapolis-based CPA and consulting firm Crowe Chizek and Company. As reported in the *Journal of Accountancy* in 1996, Crowe Chizek has developed a highly sophisticated competency scale that serves as the basis not only of its recruiting strategies but its staff development strategies as well.

A key part of the recruiting component of this strategy is a carefully structured 45-minute interview process that is expressly designed to give interviewers insights into the 12 core competencies that Crowe has identified as fundamental to its future growth and success. Candidates are asked in-depth questions about their past successes and failures and are asked to use these experiences as the basis of responses to certain hypothetical situations. Each question is designed to assess the candidate on several of the core competencies, including values and motivation.[8]

SUMMARIZE THE CONTENT

A good way to bring an interview to a comfortable close is to provide a rough summary, based on notes and recollection, of what the candidate has said about his or her background, qualifications, reasons for wanting the job, and strengths and weaknesses. Doing so accomplishes two things. First, it gives the candidate an opportunity to add new information or to clarify what might have been a miscommunication. Second, it assures the candidate that the interviewer has been a careful listener and reinforces the impression that the hiring decision will be fair.

PAY ATTENTION TO HOW QUESTIONS ARE WORDED

Companies today need to be extraordinarily careful about the way questions are actually worded during an interview. In the two groups of questions that follow, those in the first group are discriminatory; those in the second deal with the same issues but are worded in a manner that focuses on bona fide job qualifications.

Discriminatory

- Do you go to church every Sunday?
- Do you have young children at home?
- Do you intend to have a family?

Nondiscriminatory

- This job requires people to work on weekends—can you meet this requirement? (Note: Employers have the obligation, according to EEOC guidelines, to make "reasonable accommodations" for employees whose religious convictions may conflict with scheduling requirements of the business.)

- We are often under very tight deadlines that require us at times to work very late at night during the week—can you stay late on short notice?
- This job will most likely involve a great deal of travel, which means that you might be away from home three or more days at a time. Will you be able to meet this requirement?
- Is there anything that we may find out during reference checking that you'd like to talk about?

THE EIGHT HABITS OF HIGHLY EFFECTIVE INTERVIEWERS

They understand the process. Hiring managers who get the best results from interviews recognize and accept the limitations of the process. They do not base their overall assessment of the candidate solely on what happens during the interview, but instead use that experience to confirm and enhance other information, including background checks, test performance, opinions of others, and information gathered from reference sources.

They focus the process. Effective interviewers vary their interviewing strategy according to the specific type of interview they are conducting. They ask different types of questions when in the screening process than they do when the field has been narrowed down to two or three candidates.

They prepare. Effective interviewers take the time to prepare adequately for every interview they conduct. They clearly establish the criteria that will be used to evaluate candidates. They've carefully read the candidate's resume, and have noted any specific aspects of that resume that need to be addressed. They've prepared a list of key questions to ask, and have a general agenda.

They're excellent listeners. Effective interviewers understand fully that if they dominate most of the discussion, it is impossible to learn anything of value about the candidate. In short, they know how to listen—more specifically, they know how to listen *actively*. See Table 6.5 for ways to improve your listening skills.

They don't prejudge. Effective interviewers are less susceptible than most people to the pitfall of jumping to conclusions before all the information is received and evaluated.

TABLE 6.5 FIVE KEYS TO BECOMING A BETTER LISTENER

Volumes have been written about the art of listening, with most people in business readily acknowledging that very few people have truly mastered the skill. Here's a crash course in the basics of effective listening as they apply to effective interviewing.

1. *Work at it.* Never underestimate how difficult it is—and how much concentration it takes—for interviewers to give their undivided attention to what the candidate is saying. It is impossible to overstate how easy it is for the mind to wander. Keys to remember: (1) establish and maintain eye contact; (2) force yourself to listen intently to what is being said, instead of thinking about a response while the person is talking; and (3) be aware of your own body language (slumping posture) or other mannerisms (drumming of fingers, tapping of foot) that would break the connection between candidate and interviewer.
2. *Fight the tendency to respond reflexively.* Good listeners have trained themselves to overcome the impulse to formulate a response *before* the other person has had a chance to complete his or her thought. This restraint is particularly important to interviewers. From-the-hip responses not only put candidates on the defensive, they also break the flow of the conversation. The key: Become comfortable with the moment or two of silence that often separates one response from another.
3. *Fight distractions.* There are two effective ways to minimize the disruption created by distractions. The first is to take measures ahead of time (cutting off phone calls, closing the door, turning off the radio, etc.) that will minimize the likelihood of distractions. The second is to force yourself to concentrate harder whenever distractions begin to intrude. Neither is easy; both are essential.
4. *Keep note-taking to a minimum.* It's always a good idea to take notes during an interview, but the process of mechanically recording the notes shouldn't interfere with the flow of the conversation or the interviewer's ability to pay close attention to what is being said. Write down key words and ideas, and be prepared to spend 10 or 15 minutes immediately after the interview in order to write out the notes in better detail.
5. *Practice. Practice. Practice.* Becoming a better listener is largely a matter of developing better listening habits. It can start with simple things—like not trying to read the morning paper and have a conversation with somebody at the same time, or not playing a computer game while having a phone conversation. Most people who are exceptionally good listeners didn't get that way by accident: They worked at it.

They're skillful at drawing out information. Effective interviewers have developed the ability to draw information from people. They know how to put candidates at ease and have reviewed the candidate's resume, noting any topics that need to be addressed.

They're not afraid to probe or ask tough questions. Effective interviewers are not reluctant to probe more deeply for complete answers. They are able to do so, however, without alienating the person being interviewed.

They're organized. Effective interviewers stay in control of the process. In addition to having a plan, they work hard to keep the interview on track. They take careful notes throughout, and take the time after the interview to record those notes.

END POINT

Conducted properly, face-to-face interviews are the most important and most productive element of the hiring process; there is little question that a skillfully handled interview is frequently the difference between a successful hiring decision and a costly hiring mistake. The purpose of this chapter is to take a close look at what it really means to conduct a "successful" interview, and to share some of the tools and techniques that successful interviewers typically employ.

As emphasized early in this chapter, the primary challenge of job interviewing is not simply to get answers to questions but to gain a reasonably accurate sense of who the candidate is as a person and how that candidate is likely to perform on the job, given all the factors that can enhance or impede job performance. It is essential, therefore, that interviewers have a clear sense of the hiring criteria prior to the interview and that the ebb and flow of the interview be clearly keyed to those criteria. It is also essential that interviewers create the proper environment—relaxed enough to put the candidate at ease but not so relaxed that critical issues are never addressed. Questions should be asked in a way that induces the candidate to reveal attitudes and attributes that could have a strong bearing on the hiring decision, but interviewers need to keep in mind that many candidates are themselves highly skilled at the art of interviewing: They know how to give interviewers the "right" answers. Yet another attribute that separates effective interviewers from everyone else is their ability to minimize the so-called halo effect—the tendency to become overly impressed by one particular aspect of a candidate that may not have a correlation to job performance.

This chapter also emphasizes—with good reason—the importance of avoiding questions that might make the company vulnerable to charges of discrimination. Interviewers need to bear in mind at all times those issues such as race, gender, age, marital status, ethnic origin, and religion that cannot be addressed, either directly or indirectly, during interviews.

MORE READING

Barrier, Michael. "Hiring the Right People." *Nation's Business* (June 1996, vol. 84, no. 6), p. 18 (7), Reference # A18324987.

Brady, Teresa. "The Legal Horrors of Truth-in-Hiring Lawsuits." *Management Review* (October, 1996, vol. 85, no. 10), p. 53 (3).

Cherney, Lynn K. "Thirtysomething Execs Express Family Needs." *HR Focus* (September 1996, vol. 73, no. 9), p. 3 (1).

Crispell, Diane. "Computers at Home." *American Demographics* (February 1994).

Fisher, Anne. "Then I Called My Boss a Moron . . ." *Fortune* (December 23, 1996, vol. 134, no. 12), p. 243 (1).

Kirkshenberg, Seth. "Independent Contractor or Regular Employee?" *Training & Development* (April 1997).

Koonce, Richard. "Spotting Red Flags in a Job Interview." *Training & Development* (February 1997, vol. 51, no. 2), p. 15 (1).

Litvan, Laura M. "Thorny Issues in Hiring. Illegal Job Interview Topics." *Nation's Business* (April 1996, vol. 84, no. 4), p. 34 (2).

Munk, Nina and Oliver, Suzanne. "Think Fast! New Employment Interviewing Techniques: Includes Brainteasers, Guesstimates and Other Employment Tests." *Forbes* (March 24, 1997, vol. 159, no. 6), p. 146 (4).

"On the Hot Seat. Job Interview Questions That Break Superficiality." *Industry Week* (October 21, 1996, vol. 245, no. 19), p. 9 (1).

CHAPTER 7

Making the Hiring Decision

INTRODUCTION

The methods and processes that forward-thinking companies are using today to evaluate candidates are more sophisticated and more complex than ever. But the sophistication and complexity of these methods have introduced challenges that didn't exist as recently as 25 years ago. The challenge today is not simply to develop and use methods that can be reliably depended on to identify those candidates likely to become top performers. Companies must also be able to demonstrate to the satisfaction of the EEOC and other government agencies that their assessment tools do not unfairly rule out groups protected by legislation currently in effect.

Compounding this challenge is the sheer number of options available to companies who are seeking to build more sophistication and precision into their assessment and evaluation practices. Solid, empirical evidence that would clearly identify the superiority of one method over another is almost nonexistent. Consequently, companies need to rely on their own internal measures and, on occasion, on the reputation and integrity of the number of consultants and companies that are now offering candidate assessment services and products. This chapter examines today's rapidly changing assessment horizon, and presents an objective picture of the options available today and what companies need to be aware of prior to using assessment tools.

CANDIDATE ASSESSMENT OPTIONS

The question of which specific assessment option represents the most reliable predictor of job performance is a source of considerable debate among industrial psychologists and hiring professionals. There is, however, almost universal agreement on one point: The process of making accurate assessments has become far more challenging than ever before.

Reliable reference information, for one thing, has become increasingly difficult to obtain, with many companies reluctant to communicate unfavorable information about a candidate out of fear that the ex-employee will retaliate with a lawsuit. Companies today must also ensure that their assessment methods fall within the acceptable criteria—valid parameters of federal and state antidiscrimination legislation. And, finally, the changing nature of the workplace has put a premium on attributes and skills that have less to do with a candidate's ability to handle the technical aspects of a job and more to do with personality, temperament, and people skills—attributes that are exceptionally difficult to quantify, even for people trained in psychology.

Complicating this challenge is the fact that there is very little hard, reliable data that would shed light one way or the other on which specific assessment method—be it tests, selection interview evaluation, workplace task simulation, or whatever—represents the best predictor of future job performance. There are studies galore, but most fall victim to the same shortcoming: too many uncontrolled variables.

There is a great deal of talk today about "predictive validity" of tests and other assessment methods—that is, the degree to which any factor that is taken into account when a hiring decision is made correlates to future successful job performance. The truth is, however, that virtually no one to date has figured out how to study assessment methods in a way that would provide the kinds of controls needed to validate the data. If a company wanted to measure the correlation between the results of a particular test and future performance, to cite one illustration, it would have to set up a protocol in which a large group of people with widely different scores were hired to perform jobs in which the overall conditions (tasks performed, supervisor, working environment, etc.) were virtually identical. Only then could a company draw valid conclusions about whether tests were a valid predictor of future performance.

Given the paucity of empirical data, companies today are adopting what can best be described as a "multidimensional" approach to assessment. The assumption underlying this approach is that no single method or technique can be viewed as the definitive predictor of job performance. Hence, companies are relying on a combination of assessment techniques: interviews (often more than one and sometimes conducted by a variety of people), tests, and, increasingly, "orientation" procedures that double as probation periods. "There is too much at stake in hiring today to rely on any single assessment method," says Bob Bogart, executive vice president of human resources of Mutual of Omaha Companies in Omaha, Nebraska. "The old practice of relying mainly on one person's 'gut feel' based on one or two interviews is pretty much a thing of the past."[1]

DANGER!

TESTING IS SUBJECT TO SUBSTANTIAL FEDERAL, STATE, AND LOCAL REGULATIONS. THE FOLLOWING DISCUSSION OF THE RELATIVE USES AND EFFICACIES OF VARIOUS TESTS IS NOT MEANT TO IMPLY THAT ANY SUCH TEST IS LEGAL FOR ANY SPECIFIC JOB OR IN ANY STATE OR CITY. LEGAL COUNSEL SHOULD BE CONSULTED PRIOR TO USING ANY EMPLOYMENT TEST.

EMPLOYMENT TESTING: THEN AND NOW

The idea of using tests to evaluate candidates seems logical and harmless enough on the surface, but preemployment testing has emerged as one of the most controversial and vigorously debated issues in hiring. Testing is subject to substantial federal, state, and local regulation.

Few question the theoretical rationale of testing—that if a test is carefully designed and properly interpreted, its results can be a reasonably accurate predictor of job performance, especially when the results are combined with impressions gathered during a job interview. The debate has to do more with the standards that should be used to measure the validity of a test—and the moral and legal implications of using certain tests.

It's hardly a new debate, and it is not likely to ease in the near future. Preemployment testing has figured one way or another in the selection practices of business and government agencies since the early 1900s. It has been extensively used by the military since World War I, and by the 1960s it was not unusual to find major companies using a battery of skills, intelligence, and personality tests in both their prescreening and selection procedures. See Table 7.1 for a look at some of the more common tests.

The picture changed dramatically, though, in the 1970s, following a historic U.S. Supreme Court decision known as *Griggs v. Duke Power Company.* Duke Power, not unlike many companies at the time, had two recruitment and promotion policies that in the Court's view arbitrarily limited employment and promotion opportunities for minorities. For one thing, it insisted that all candidates have at least a high school diploma, and it obliged all employees seeking to move from the labor department of the company to higher levels to pass two "professionally developed" personnel tests. Neither of these requirements would have been a problem if the proportion of minorities on the company's payroll (and in higher-level positions) had been consistent with the proportion of minori-

TABLE 7.1 A CAPSULE LOOK AT THE MOST COMMONLY ADMINISTERED TESTS

Type of test	What it measures
Aptitude	An individual's capacity or potential to learn the skills required to perform a particular job
Psychomotor tests	Physical capabilities, such as strength, hand-eye coordination, and visual perception
Intelligence tests	Raw intellectual capacity: the ability to reason, process information, and solve problems
Proficiency and skills test	The skills actually required to do a particular task
Psychology and personality tests	Personality traits (flexibility, assertiveness, confidence, etc.) and psychological tendencies
Integrity tests	Character, truthfulness, and conscientiousness
Polygraph	Truthfulness of answers about background and skills

ties in the local labor force, but such was not the case. And because the company was unable to prove to the Court's satisfaction that either of these requirements were directly related to the "safe and efficient operation of the company," the Court ruled that the tests were illegal.[2]

The effect of the Supreme Court's ruling in the Griggs case was immediate and dramatic. Never having gone to the expense of determining whether the tests they were using were indeed "valid" by the standard that the Supreme Court had established in its ruling, most companies decided to simply eliminate the tests from their selection procedures—much to the chagrin of psychologists, consultants, and hiring professionals who had developed many of the tests and had been relying on them for years.

In recent years, however, as test development has become more sophisticated, the testing pendulum is now moving in the opposite direction, and the use of tests is once again on the rise, albeit with controls that didn't exist prior to the 1970s. Some of the best known companies in the United States—Procter & Gamble, Kraft General Foods, and AT&T, to name just three—rely a good deal on testing.[3] Each of these companies has gone to considerable lengths to ensure that the tests it uses do not violate the EEOC guidelines or the Americans with Disabilities Act. At Kraft, for instance, much of the testing that the company conducts is under the supervision of the same department responsible for the company's diversity program.[4]

But, legalities notwithstanding, employment testing raises other nettlesome and unresolved issues. The primary concern relates to the predictive validity of these tests—whether the results of the tests are accurate predictors of future job performance. Anecdotal information abounds, and there are, to be sure, many companies today whose hiring managers swear by the validity and usefulness of different types of tests, particularly those designed to measure personality, integrity, and motivation.

According to a 1995 report in *Supervision* magazine, the turnover rate at Hannaford Brothers Company, a Maine-based grocery store chain, dropped to "next to nothing" after the company began using a multiple-choice screening test that had been developed by Scheig Associates of Gig Harbor, Washington, one of a rapidly growing number of human resources consulting firms that specializes in preemployment testing programs. And a study conducted in 1992 by the University of Manchester in England found that companies relying on employment tests reported savings in their "human capital costs" of between 15 and 25 percent.[5]

The arguments against testing, on the other hand, cannot be arbitrarily dismissed. As opponents of testing are quick to point out, the science that underlies employment testing is shaky at best and nonexistent at worst, particularly when it comes to those tests that purport to shed light on a candidate's personality and temperament. A handful of these tests—most notably the Rorschach test and the Thematic Apperception Test (TAT)—have been routinely used in clinical situations for decades and are generally accepted as valid ways to measure personality traits. But tests like Rorschach and TAT need to be interpreted by professionals who have the appropriate training and background. Most of the personality tests being used in business today are of the "do-it-yourself" variety. In some instances, the tests are customized to a specific job task (sales, for instance), and, less commonly, to the singularity of a company or a specific marketplace. Customizing tests, however, can be costly, which is why most of the companies that employ tests in their hiring procedures are using generic, off-the-shelf tests that are easy and convenient to administer and to score.

How reliable and valid are these commercial tests? The answer depends on whose opinion is being sought. Companies that develop and market the tests maintain that they are a reliable and valuable tool in the hiring process and seem to have no shortage of satisfied customers to back up the claim. Like it or not, these companies argue, personality plays a big part in determining not only how well a candidate will perform on a job but how easily he or she will be able to adapt to the corporate culture. And well-designed tests, their producers maintain, are a much more reliable and objective source of information on the candidate's personality than the subjective judgments of the average interviewer.

Opponents of testing don't agree. The American Civil Liberties Union, for instance, has been arguing since the mid-1960s that the use of personality and psychological tests in hiring represents an "invasion of privacy." As Lewis Maltby, director of workplace rights for the ACLU, once explained it, "The law is fuzzy at best. Psychological testing ought to be a limited process, and it goes much farther than it should. The employer doesn't need to know an employee's deepest secrets."[6]

The bigger issue, though, is validity. Most industrial psychologists scoff at the very notion that a multiple-choice test, regardless of how well it has been designed, can yield reliable information about what makes candidates tick. Clever job seekers, they argue, can manipulate the answers to create whatever impression they want, and even if that isn't the case, there are simply too many variables to allow simplistic cause-and-effect connections between test answers and actual job performance.

See Table 7.2 for some areas to research when considering an off-the-shelf test.

EVALUATING EMPLOYMENT TESTS: A CRASH COURSE

The ability to decide whether a particular test can enhance a company's selection process in a manner that is both cost effective and legally sound requires at least a rudimentary understanding of the concepts and terminology that test developers use in describing the reliability of their tests. The following is a crash course in some of the terms frequently used by testing professionals. The more familiar a hiring manager is with these terms, the easier it will be to decide which tests have the most reliable track record.

Average. The arithmetic mean of any group of numbers, arrived at by adding up all the numbers and dividing that sum by the number of items enumerated. The average of the five following numbers—1, 3, 4, 7, 25—would be 8 [the sum (40) divided by 5]. Evaluators need to realize when reviewing promotional literature that the term *average* isn't necessarily representative of how most of the people involved in a particular study performed.

TABLE 7.2 FIVE CRITICAL STEPS TO TAKE BEFORE USING AN OFF-THE-SHELF TEST

- Investigate the credentials and reputation of the company that has developed and published the test.
- Verify what specific traits the test is meant to measure and make sure there is a close match between those traits and the hiring criteria.
- Make doubly certain that the tests are not biased against any group.
- Verify that the test has been certified by a reputable and independent organization.
- Talk to people from companies that have similar job requirements and are currently using tests.

Median. The middle number in a group of numbers. The median in the sequence 1, 3, 4, 7, 25 would be 4. Knowing the median helps to clarify the practical significance of "average."

Correlation. The statistical relationship between two variables in any test measurement situation. If there is a discernible pattern—i.e., increases in one variable are mirrored by increases in the other—the two variables are in correlation with one another. (Note: the fact that a correlation exists between two variables does not necessarily indicate a cause-and-effect relationship. The relationship could simply be coincidental.)

Variance. The width (or narrowness) of the gap that exists among the individual results of a single parameter being measured. The wider the variance (or scatter), the less valid the parameter becomes as a predictor. For large samples, variance is arrived at by determining the mean (i.e., midpoint) and averaging the square of each value's deviation from the mean.

Standard deviation. The statistical measure used to define the degree of variance. It is calculated by taking the square root of the variance.

Reliability. The most common way of measuring the reliability of a test is to administer it to a group of people, record the results, and then, after a short period (a week or two), re-administer it. Assuming that no learning has taken place in the interim, a reliable test will produce the same general results the second time around that it did the first time. One of the key factors in reliability is the number of variables: The fewer the variables in any given situation, the more reliable the method is likely to be. Reliability is probably one of the most notable strengths of the most common standard tests used in employee evaluation. It is one of the principal shortcomings of the selection interview as a fundamental hiring tool.

Predictive validity. The degree to which test results scores correlate with future job performance.

In evaluating any "validated" tests, there are four issues to be considered.

1. Do the test results really reflect mastery of the skill being tested?

2. Does passing the test depend on unrelated factors?
3. Are the skills measured by the test required for the job?
4. Is the passing grade set at the right level for the job?

It is important to keep all four of these requirements in mind when evaluating any test. Standardized tests that are marketed as being "validated" can usually only be relied on to satisfy the first two requirements listed above. The last two requirements must be considered separately in light of the company's specific job description.

PUT MENTAL ABILITY IN PERSPECTIVE

The general intelligence level or mental ability of a candidate—as measured by IQ—has traditionally been viewed as an across-the-board predictor, the theory being that the better a person is at processing information and solving problems, the easier he or she will be to train. But there is one aspect of this otherwise logical guideline that needs to be addressed. While differences in intelligence may be a valid predictor of how quickly a person will learn a particular job, they don't necessarily determine how effectively the person will perform once the job has been learned. Some studies suggest, in fact, that in certain types of jobs, "slower" learners actually perform better because as they're not as likely to get bored.

ASSURING THE INTEGRITY OF THE DECISION-MAKING PROCESS

Regardless of the source of the information used to evaluate candidates—whether it comes from test scores, interview assessments, or resume information—the process of actually making the hiring decisions needs to be carried out with understanding and discipline. As in any decision-making situation, people should do their best to insulate themselves from factors that are extraneous to the specific decision at hand. It is important, for example, that the hiring manager isn't unduly influenced by a sense of urgency to fill a position. Managers need to keep reminding themselves that a bad short-term decision will only make things worse in the long run. Here are five other decision-making guidelines.

1. *Stay focused on the hiring criteria:* The single most important point in assessment is to make sure the process is driven by the hiring criteria of the job and not by such criteria as appearance, a "great personality," or common interests, for example.
2. *Make sure the assessment parameters are appropriately weighted:* The true art of assessment lies in the ability to attach appropriate evaluative weight to each criterion used in the process. Weighting means that in addition to listing criteria, an attempt is made to establish the relative importance of each.
3. *Don't ignore "gut" feelings:* "Gut"—an intuitive sense that the candidate is either "right or wrong" for a job, all other factors notwithstanding—should never take automatic precedence over reasonably objective evidence that runs counter to the feeling, but it should not be undervalued, either. The litmus test: whether gut feelings in the past have produced a consistent record of successful hires or out-and-out disasters. Savvy hiring professionals always play the odds.
4. *Don't become too absorbed with the candidate's background "on paper:"* A major pitfall in hiring is to become impressed with credentials to the detriment of evaluating other critical aspects. An applicant might have worked in the industry with an ideally suited specialization, or have a degree from a very prestigious college. But he or she may, on further analysis or reference checking, be a ruthless manager or poor team player, making this person the wrong choice.
5. *Be wary of the "expectations" effect and other timing pitfalls:* Robert Half International surveys have shown that, as a rule, the first person interviewed for a job is less likely to be hired than the last person, even though there may be no discernable differences in their qualifications. The most likely explanation: With no

Stellar Performer: **Microtraining Plus**

When people apply at Microtraining Plus, a Norwalk, Connecticut, company that specializes in Macintosh training, CEO David Knise asks them to do something people don't normally do during a job interview. He has them make an hour-long presentation to his eight-member staff on any topic other than computers. "We're hiring people for ability to get up in front of six people they don't know and make a presentation," Knise told *Inc.* magazine in an article published in June 1996. "So we want to make sure that people know how to organize their thoughts and they have reasonable command of a classroom." Knise notes that he pays particularly close attention to how candidates respond to disruptive participants and whether the applicants play specifically to him or to others in the audience. "The more confident people," he says, "don't play to me as much." Knise credits this novel selection tool as the main reason his employees later receive high written evaluations from customers.[7]

frame of reference, expectations for persons interviewed earlier in the process tend to be higher than the expectations that exist near the end of the process. Consequently, relatively strong candidates interviewed early often seem weak, while weaker applicants interviewed later seem strong. Interviewers need to recognize these pitfalls and must do their best to avoid the distortions that can result from them.

THE RELATIONSHIP BETWEEN CANDIDATE BACKGROUND AND JOB PERFORMANCE

As discussed earlier, studies designed to establish correlations between specific information in a candidate's background and post-hiring job performance have failed to yield any data that would have practical significance in typical hiring situations. One possible exception, however, is a study that was conducted in the early 1990s by Robert Lavigna, who reported his findings in *Public Personnel Management.* Embedded in Lavigna's results are implications that have relevance to a wide range of hiring situations.[8]

Lavigna was interested in five of the most commonly scrutinized factors in the backgrounds of candidates as these applied to one group of would-be employees in particular—college graduates seeking entry-level positions in a large, state-run agency. The study involved 564 college graduates: 55 percent were women, 22 percent were minorities. Roughly half the group had graduate degrees.

The factors Lavigna was seeking to measure as predictors of future job performance were the following.

- Grade point average in college
- Level of degree (graduate or advanced)
- Major field of study
- Reputation of college attended
- Extent of previous work experience

Lavigna wanted to know how hiring managers viewed each of these factors as predictors of future job performance, and how each of these factors correlated with actual job performance as measured by on-the-job performance appraisals. The premise was that most hiring managers place too much importance on factors that ultimately have little or no relationship to future job performance.

The findings of the study confirmed Lavigna's suspicions. The recruiters and hiring managers surveyed felt all five factors were valid predictors of future job performance. The results, though, indicated otherwise. Following is a rundown of what Lavigna discovered, along with a discussion of how these findings might apply to hiring situations in general.

Grade point average. Of the five factors measured, grade point average (GPA) turned out to be the single most reliable predictor of job performance—and by a substantial margin.

Reputation of college. The reputation of the college an employee had attended showed almost no correlation (as Lavigna had hypothesized) with job performance. The performance appraisals of students who came from the "top" colleges were not significantly higher than the appraisals of those from less prestigious colleges.

Degree earned. Here again, as Lavigna predicted, the fact that a candidate had an advanced degree seemed to have little impact on job performance. This finding, incidentally, confirmed earlier studies showing that educational level is a relatively poor predictor of job performance in entry-level positions.

Major field of study. Although the applicant's major field of study was found to be an important factor in the hiring process, it had little statistical bearing on the quality of the job performance appraisal. Generalists performed as well as people who had specialized in certain fields.

Previous work experience. Contrary to what one would normally expect, the extent of an applicant's previous work experience only marginally correlated to above-average job performance. Those employees who'd had previous experience tended to outperform their counterparts early on, but those with little or no experience rapidly caught up.

Lavigna was quick to warn against the danger of overgeneralizing his findings. He reminded readers, for instance, that all the applicants had high GPAs to begin with, and also pointed out that the jobs these young graduates took involved tasks that were not that far removed from what the employees had been doing in college. Nevertheless, Lavigna suggested that the following can be gleaned from his study, flawed and limited though it may have been.

- All things being equal, high-performing graduates of colleges that have lesser reputations will perform as well as graduates from "top" schools.
- Unless there is a direct connection between the field of study and the job, an advanced degree cannot be viewed as an accurate predictor of job performance.
- Everything else being equal, previous job experience is a greater predictor of how quickly people will get up to speed in a new job than how effectively they will perform once they've acclimated.

INTEGRITY TESTS: TO CATCH A THIEF

When they were first marketed in the late 1970s, integrity tests were viewed skeptically by most hiring professionals because it was difficult for people to believe that candidates would be truthful enough in their answers to make the tests valid. In the early 1990s, however, three University of Iowa industrial psychologists—Deniz S. Ones, Chockalingam Viswesvaran, and Frank L. Schmidt—did an intensive analysis of more than 40 tests with data from a half-million test participants. The thesis was that the tests, when properly administered, actually worked. As reporter Daniel Seligman noted in a *Fortune* article that ran shortly before the Iowa psychologists published their findings in the *Journal of Applied Psychology,* these tests had "quite substantial criterion validates." Test results correlated significantly and positively with supervisors' subsequent reports on the behavior being predicted." As such, the integrity tests were judged to be "reasonably effective" at identifying candidates with "low integrity."

Why do such tests work? According to Seligman's report, dishonest people have a paradoxical tendency to be forthcoming when they are asked direct questions about misdeeds they may have committed while on their last jobs. It may be, Seligman suggests, that people taking the tests may "half-suspect" that their prospective employers are already aware of problems the candidates may have had in previous jobs, or it could be that thieves have a propensity to believe that "everybody does it."[9] Nevertheless, legal counsel with expertise in local employment laws should be consulted prior to the use of any given test.

AN INSIDE LOOK AT ASSESSMENT CENTERS

Assessment center is a term that is sometimes used to describe a specific method of assessment or the actual place where the assessment occurs. The idea behind the concept, in any case, is the same. Applicants are brought to a specific place and are given a series of tasks, tests, or exercises to perform—during which they are observed by specially trained assessors.

The assessment center as a selection technique was originally developed by the military during World War II, but the company most responsible for its early development was AT&T, which developed the combination of activities and many of the assessment concepts that constitute the basic model on which most assessment centers today are based.

In a typical assessment center process, candidates are asked to go through a series of so-called "in-basket" exercises—that is, actual tasks that they could well be performing on their first day on the job (see Table 7.3). In addition, there are paper-and-pencil tests, group exercises, leaderless discussions, and role-playing exercises. Every company has its own variation of the process. At the Hamilton Standard Commercial Aircraft Elec-

TABLE 7.3 TYPICAL ASSESSMENT CENTER EXERCISES

- Applicants are given a stack of memos and letters and asked to sort them out, taking action on some and delegating others.
- Applicants are gathered into groups in which each individual is asked to make a brief presentation to convince other group members to allocate limited resources to a specific cause that is championed by the presenter.

tronics Division of United Technologies, many of the front-line employees are actively involved in the center's activities. On any given Saturday, as many as 50 employees will come to the assessment center and join with job applicants in a teaming exercise whose objective is to develop a model airplane. Current employees conduct both technical and general interviews with applicants, and they meet afterward as a group to discuss each candidate.[10]

Still other companies have expanded the scope of the assessment center concept to include training as well as assessing. Sprint, for instance, sends many of its candidates for supervisor, manager, or director positions to its University of Excellence training and development centers in the Kansas City, Missouri, area. The typical program lasts three days, during which time candidates go through a series of role-playing exercises that simulate the kind of situations they are likely to encounter once on the job.[11]

The exercises are carefully structured (actors and consultants often play the parts of disgruntled customers or employees) to make the exercise as life-like as possible. As Sprint's project manager of employee development explained it in a 1995 article in *Sales and Marketing Management,* "We want to see if the person can solve problems by being empathetic, by helping people reach their own conclusions, not telling them what to do."

Most of the studies that have been done on assessment centers have painted a generally favorable picture of the role the centers play in fostering successful hiring decisions. Validity coefficients—the principal measure of any assessment—have been as high as 0.60 in some cases, an unusually high number. The reason for this impressive success rate, according to organizational development authorities, is that the focus throughout the process is on observable behavior—what candidates are actually *doing* in potential work situations as opposed to what they are *saying they would do* as they're being interviewed in an office. The main variable in the results of assessment, according to most studies, is the level of training and expertise among the people who serve as assessors. The principal drawback is the cost, time, and effort required to set up a center, develop the exercises, and operate it efficiently on a regular basis.

BE CAREFUL ABOUT DRUG TESTING

DANGER!

Drug testing is subject to substantial restriction, much of which is imposed by court decisions on a state-by-state basis. This area is changing so rapidly that any discussion of the legalities would be out of date almost immediately. The best advice is to consult with legal counsel before implementing any drug testing program.

There are two ways to test for drugs. The most common method is enzyme multiplied immunoassay, more commonly referred to as *urinalysis* or *urine sampling.* A more recent—and many believe, more effective—test involves the sampling of hair and is known as hair follicle testing.

Neither method is ideal. Urinalysis is widely accepted and relatively inexpensive. But it has drawbacks.

- It doesn't usually detect drugs that were taken more than three days prior to the test (traces of the drug have generally left the system by then).
- It frequently produces "false positives"—results that are produced by over-the-counter drugs or legal prescription drugs.
- In order for the test to be administered, there must be a same-sex observer present to verify the source of the sample.

Hair follicle testing is generally regarded as the more accurate of the two methods. This is because drugs become permanently locked into the hair follicle, making it possible to determine not only that a candidate has been taking drugs, but also, with a fair degree of accuracy, when the drugs were taken and whether an individual's drug use is on the increase or decline. Another advantage is that hair is a much more stable testing medium: It can be shipped and stored more easily and conveniently than urine. But hair follicle testing has its drawbacks as well. The two most common follow.

- At present, it's about three times as expensive as urine testing.
- The preferred procedure—plucking individual strands of hair so that the roots can be tested—can be painful.[12]

There is a growing feeling among employment law specialists that hair follicle testing represents a growing trend.

TIP

ENHANCING PREDICTIVE VALIDITY

The predictive validity of a test is the degree to which the results of the test correlate with job performance. It is an extremely difficult variable to control given all the conditions that need to be met.

But hiring professionals seeking to build more predictive validity into their tests can enhance their chances of achieving this goal by doing their best to ensure that the following conditions are met.

- Applicant tests are administered under the same conditions.
- Applicants (for at least one group) are hired regardless of how well they score on the parameter whose predictive validity is being measured.
- Steps are taken to ensure that all applicants receive the same basic training and orientation and work under the same general conditions.
- Definitive success criteria are set for the job.
- Correlation is measured between job performance and test scores of all applicants.

THE HEAD, HANDS, AND SHOULDERS APPROACH

When marketing communication strategist Arthur Einstein was a partner in the advertising agency Lord Geller, Frederico, and Einstein, he developed a "people-picking formula" that he insists can work in every industry. Einstein says that when he was evaluating candidates he made it a point to look for "heads, hands, and shoulders." Translation:

Head: His estimate of how smart the person was.

Hands: His estimate of how skillful the person was with respect to the job at hand.

Shoulders: His estimate of how much responsibility the person could handle.[13]

GAMES OF CHANCE

Can a candidate's likelihood of success on the job be predicted on the basis of how successfully he or she plays certain games of chance? In 1995, *Forbes* magazine decided to investigate this question and came up with some intriguing observations. The most noteworthy observation: Some of the best-known corporate personalities in America—people like Carl Icahn, Warren Buffet, and Lawrence Tisch—all happen to be accomplished game players.

No surprise, either, according to Philip E. Ross, who wrote the article. Games like poker, bridge, and backgammon, he points out, reward many of the same qualities that underlie successful performance in business. Chief among them are "discipline, memory, coolness under pressure, psychological insightfulness, a readiness to stick to a strategy even when it produces losing streaks in the short run, and rapid and intuitive calculation of probabilities—of spotting opportunities and balancing risks against rewards."

One key player on Wall Street, according to Ross, believes so strongly in the connection between the ability to play certain games well and perform well in business that when hiring people he goes out of his way to seek out accomplished bridge players. The man's name is Michael Becker. He is a trader on the American Stock Exchange and is himself a champion bridge player. Becker maintains, according to Ross, that some 20 percent of the traders on the American Stock Exchange are accomplished games players, and the reason Becker can make that assertion is that he and his partner personally hired and trained those 90 people. Says Becker, "I can unqualifiedly say that the people I've trained have outperformed the others."[14]

END POINT

This chapter addresses some of the methods—apart from the employment interview—that organizations can use to get a clearer and more objective view of the strengths and weaknesses of job candidates. It focuses in particular on the growing role that testing now plays in the selection process.

The old-fashioned method of basing hiring decisions solely on "gut" feelings is a dangerous and costly proposition. Instead, companies today are adopting what can best be described as a multidimensional approach to candidate assessment, including interviews, orientation periods, and testing.

There are many different types of hiring-related tests available today, ranging from simple skills examinations that measure proficiency in a particular job function to tests that purportedly develop an accurate profile of a candidate. Many hiring managers feel that certain types of examinations can be predictors of how a candidate will perform on the job. Opponents of employment testing, however, maintain that the science underlying it is unreliable, particularly when it comes to those tests that claim to reveal a candidate's personality and temperament.

Consequently, employment testing remains a controversial issue, and organizations seeking to incorporate this evaluation method into their hiring procedures should approach it with great care. It is essential, for example, that any tests used are not biased against any group, and it is equally important that the tests be keyed to factors that are valid predictors of job performance success. Legal counsel should be consulted prior to conducting any employment testing, as it is subject to federal, state, and local regulations.

MORE READING

Applegate, Jane. "Bad Workers Got You Down? Better Screening Might Help." *Denver Business Journal* (September 16, 1994, vol. 46, no. 1), p. 24 (1).

Brady, Teresa. "Coming and Going: The Regulations that Make the Pre-Employment Process Difficult Do not Apply to Exit Interviews." *Management Review* (August 1996, vol. 85, no. 8), p. 10 (3).

Brotherton, Phaedra. "Exit Interview Can Provide a Reality Check." *HR Magazine* (August 1996, vol. 41, no. 8), p. 45 (5).

Fairley, Juliette. "It's Not Your Father's Job Market Anymore: Interviewing is More Intense and Rigorous than Ever Before." *Black Enterprise* (July 1995, vol. 25, no. 12), p. 66 (1).

Flynn, Gillian. "Score A+ Employees With Pre-Employment Testing. Survival Guide for Recruitment 1995–1996." *Workforce* magazine, formerly known as *Personnel Journal* (August 1995, vol. 74, no. 8), p. S6 (4).

Frazee, Valerie. "Do Your Job-Applicant Tests Make the Grade?" *Workforce* magazine, formerly known as *Personnel Journal* (August 1996, vol. 75, no. 8), p. S16 (2).

Greenlaw, Paul S. and Sanne S. Jensen. "Race-Norming and the Civil Rights Act of 1991." *Public Personnel Management* (Spring 1996, vol. 25, no. 1), p. 13 (12).

Kennedy, Marilyn Moats. "Do You Really Want to Know? Exit Interviews, and What Can Managers Do With What They Learn From Them." in "Up the Organization" column. *Across the Board* (October 1996, vol. 33, no. 9), p. 53 (2).

Lavigna, Robert J. "Innovation in Recruiting and Hiring: Attracting the Best and Brightest to Wisconsin State Government." *Public Personnel Management* (Winter 1996, vol. 25, no. 4), p. 423 (15).

Murphy, Kevin R. "Why Pre-Employment Alcohol Testing is Such a Bad Idea." *Business Horizons* (September/October 1995, vol. 38, no. 5), p. 69 (6).

Pratkanis, Anthony and Elliot Aronson. *Age of Propaganda: The Everyday Use and Abuse of Persuasion.* New York: W. H. Freeman and Company, 1991.

"Pre-Employment Testing Programs." *Supervision* (October 1995, vol. 56, no. 10), p. 17 (2).

Starkey, Malcolm. "Testing the Tests." *Management Today* (May 1992), p. 76 (3).

Wendover, Robert W. *Smart Hiring For Your Business.* Small Business Sourcebooks, 1993, p. 131.

CHAPTER

Nailing Things Down

INTRODUCTION

It is one thing to make the "best choice" when interviewing and evaluating candidates, but it is something else to successfully hire the chosen person. Two key steps remain. The first is checking the candidate's references as thoroughly as possible. The second is making the formal offer and, if necessary, negotiating the terms of that offer. Neither of these steps can be taken for granted. Both can factor heavily into whether the person hired will turn out to be a successful and productive employee. This chapter examines these areas, focusing on the challenges that have arisen in each over the past decade.

REFERENCE CHECKING: TODAY'S "DOUBLE BIND" AND HOW IT GOT THAT WAY

Reference checking used to be a fairly routine procedure—a simple matter of getting in touch with a candidate's former employer, verifying a few facts, getting some feedback on the candidate's strengths and weaknesses, and making sure there weren't any skeletons in the candidate's closet that could create serious problems once he or she had been hired. Not everybody who was asked to provide reference feedback was equally forthcoming, of course, but companies seeking reference information could usually take for granted that what they were hearing from a candidate's former employer was the truth.

Unfortunately, today the reference-checking aspect of hiring doesn't work the way it used to. The result is that companies in increasing numbers now find themselves between the proverbial rock and hard place. Getting reliable reference information about candidates who are seriously being considered for employment is as important as ever—especially in light of recent lawsuits that have found companies liable for the violent actions of employees whose backgrounds had not been investigated thoroughly enough prior to hiring. At the same time, though, the fear of retaliatory suits from disgruntled ex-employees has led most American companies (the larger ones, in particular) to adopt tight-lipped reference feedback policies that make it extremely difficult, if not impossible, to get the kind of information that employers need to protect themselves from being sued for "negligent" hiring practices.

The roots of today's reference-checking quandary date back to the mid-1970s. It was then that a series of court rulings gave individuals the right to sue their ex-employers for libel, slander, or defamation if it could be shown that the ex-employer had made false representations during reference-seeking communication and that those representations had resulted in the individual not being hired.

Civil libertarians and right-to-privacy groups had been arguing for years that individuals needed this kind of legal muscle to protect themselves from ex-employers who might tell lies simply out of spite; but even those who had been lobbying the most strongly for more of this kind of protection were taken aback by some of the huge settlements that plaintiffs who brought such suits were being awarded.

In one case, settled in 1985, a Houston insurance salesman who'd been fired from his previous job was awarded $1.9 million when a private investigator impersonating a would-be employer was told by the salesman's employer that the man was a "classic sociopath," a "zero," and someone who was "lacking in scruples."[1] That award, though, was minimal compared to the $60.2 million that a former sales rep from NEC was awarded when an electronic industry newsletter had quoted company officials as saying that the sales rep had misused funds and mismanaged his office.[2]

The publicity surrounding those high-ticket early rulings created a pervasive sense of concern among companies throughout the country, and that concern is as palpable today as it was 10 years ago. As it happens, the number of instances over the past 15 years in which companies have suffered financially because of statements issued during reference checking is minuscule when viewed against the hundreds of millions of hirings that have occurred during the same period.

Still, most companies today—large companies in particular—have instituted policies that make it difficult, if not impossible, to get useful and reliable reference information. Line managers are frequently under orders to refer all reference requests to the human resources department, where standard procedure is to give out only the most routine of information, such as dates of employment and last position held. The unfortunate result is that employers are often denied access to information that would have a significant bearing on their hiring decision—on occasion, with disastrous consequences.

So much for the bad news. The good news is that the challenge of getting reliable reference information is slowly easing, according to most human resources specialists. Because everyone recognizes how important it is that employers be able to share information about problem employees, more than 20 states, including Florida, California, Oklahoma, and Louisiana, have passed legislation that offers some protection to companies that communicate "good-faith" reference information. It's likely that similar legislation will be on the books in most states within the next five years. However, such legislation may not provide much protection from litigation as suits focus on whether the company acted in "good faith," which is a subjective term.

But even with this legislation in place, most companies are still playing it close to the vest when it comes to responding openly to reference requests. In a survey conducted in the mid-1990s by the Society for Human Resources Management (SHRM), 63 percent of the more than 1300 human resources employees contacted reported that either they or someone in their departments had withheld information about former employees for fear of lawsuits. More alarmingly, some 40 percent expressed the view that even when information is factual, human resources professionals should refuse to share it with prospective employers.[3]

All of which explains why reference checking today can be so time-consuming and frustrating, and why some executives view it as a futile, cumbersome task. Nevertheless, reference checking represents what may well be a company's number one defense against making the most serious and costly kinds of hiring mistakes. Difficult as the challenge is, references need to be checked—and checked thoroughly. Table 8.1 presents some strategies to achieve this.

HOW COMPANIES ARE RESPONDING

Recent legislation notwithstanding, it is generally recognized that taking the conventional, going-through-channels approach to checking references is not the best way to obtain useful information—especially when the previous employer is a major corporation. It is no surprise, then, that resourceful employers over the past several years have been responding to the challenge in any number of ways.

One trend that is clearly on the rise is the use of outside reference-gathering investigators. Sometimes referred to as *resume verifiers,* these

TABLE 8.1 SEVEN WAYS TO GET AROUND THE REFERENCE-CHECK BIND

With reliable reference information more difficult to obtain than ever, companies today can no longer rely on conventional reference-checking methods. Here are some ways to enhance the quality of the reference information that is gathered.

Make reference verification a precondition of hiring. There is no law that prevents a company from making some form of reference verification a precondition of hiring, as long as the information being verified is job related and doesn't violate discrimination laws.

Get a written waiver from the candidate. Written waivers that grant the employers the right to check references may not completely protect a company from legal action, but the requirement does provide a first defense and could lead candidates who have something to hide to withdraw from consideration on their own accord.

Network to get references. When you do find a responsive reference, be sure to ask him or her for more references within the organization, and do the same with each person you speak with to increase your chances of getting more useful information. If checking on an entry-level candidate, consider contacting former professors. Don't overlook your own network of contacts—a friend, relative, or business associate may know the candidate and be able to provide input.

Offer the former employer a written waiver of responsibility. Before asking a company to provide reference information, have a waiver ready that provides a release from future liability should the candidate create problems in the new job. Here again, it's questionable whether such a document could stand up in court, but it could pry some truthful information from companies that would otherwise withhold it.

Look beyond the obvious. The more people who are contacted for references, the less likely it is that someone with something serious to hide will slip through the net. Most hiring professionals recommend that three to five references be reached for each employee. The best people to contact are former bosses, but peers and subordinates shouldn't be overlooked. The least reliable people to approach: "personal" references.

Don't delegate the job. An excellent rule of thumb to follow is to have the reference-checking process personally conducted by the supervisor to whom the candidate will report. There are several reasons why this approach makes sense. The most important is that the person asked to comment on a former employee is more likely to be candid with his or her counterpart at another company than with someone who is simply handling the project on an administrative basis.

Consult "company-friendly" references. Attempts should be made, if possible, to get in touch with people who know the candidate but have more allegiance to the company than to the candidate. These contacts might include vendors, current employees, or other business associates. These references may not be able to comment directly on a candidate's work practices, but they could contribute other valuable information.

companies or individuals can be hired for a specific situation or can work as ongoing consultants. The specific methods used by this new breed of hiring specialist range from the mundane—going through public court records to see whether a prospective employee has ever been arrested—to more sophisticated and legally regulated tactics such as credit record analysis and, hard though it may be to believe, reviewing the kinds of books a candidate takes from the library, the types of vacations the candidate enjoys, and the types of videos he or she rents. The fees for doing this work vary from $75 or so for a simple background check to several thousand dollars for more detailed investigations.

The rationale for using outside specialists to check references is that they are more thoroughly trained and equipped than business people in general to unearth substantial amounts of information. The number of companies using these specialists is difficult to estimate. New amendments to the Fair Credit Reporting Act require most companies to obtain the consent of candidates before using outside sources to investigate potential employees. But the mere fact that the number of companies that now occupy this niche in the hiring process is rapidly increasing would indicate that the demand for these services is brisk.

Companies should be advised, however, that in the event their outside consultants violate laws in their investigative efforts, the companies who've hired them may be held liable. It is essential, therefore, that companies do a thorough job of researching the integrity and professionalism of the firms or individuals they hire and be thoroughly versed in all the legalities that relate to the practice.

Yet another trend in reference checking—and one that embodies far less risk—is to follow the lead of Sinclair Oil. According to a report in the December 1995 issue of *HR Magazine,* Sinclair Oil has instituted a "no-reference, no-hire" policy that puts the burden of getting accurate reference information on the candidate. Sinclair's HR director, John Goodwin, explained the rationale behind his company's policy by pointing out that "if the applicants really want the job, then they'll go back to the [previous] employer and ask for a reference." Goodwin added that this requirement weeds out two different types of applicants: (1) those who aren't really interested in the job, and (2) those who know that the reference they get won't be flattering.[4]

DON'T SHY AWAY FROM TOUGH QUESTIONS

There is an understandable tendency among people seeking reference information to only want to hear the "good" news about a candidate, and not to probe deeply enough about problems. Keep in mind that one of the main purposes of obtaining reference information is to prevent hiring mistakes. Failing to ask penetrating questions defeats the purpose of the process. See Table 8.2 for a list of good questions.

USE PERSISTENCE TO UNCOVER VALUABLE REFERENCE DATA

Jack Janco takes it for granted that when he calls companies to check references on a potential employee, he'll run into a stone wall. Janco is the director of human resources for Clough, Harbour & Associates, a consulting engineering firm in Albany, New York, and he has learned through personal experience that persistence inevitably pays off when calls are made to references. "Usually when I call for references," Janco told a magazine reporter from *Personnel Journal* in 1994, "I'll get the standard answer: 'We're sorry but it's our company policy to only give information on last position held and dates of hire.' But I don't give up. I generally say, 'I understand that you can't talk about the person, but if you could, what would you tell me?' " It may seem too simple, but Janco says he gets his information. "Nine times out of ten, it works," he says. "First they laugh, then they start talking."[5]

TABLE 8.2 ASKING THE RIGHT QUESTIONS

The specific questions that should be asked of references will generally depend on how cooperative and open the reference is. Remember, though, that even the most tight-lipped former employers are usually willing to surrender routine information about a candidate. Here's a list of questions divided into two categories: obvious ones that will help to verify that candidates have been truthful in their resume information and their answers to interview questions, and tougher ones that some reference sources will be willing to answer and others won't. The first group of questions do not lend themselves to probing. The second group, however, can be the basis of substantive conversations, as long as each question is asked in a nonthreatening manner.

Routine

- What were the dates of employment?
- What was the person's last position?
- What were the basic responsibilities of that position?
- To whom did the person report?
- What was the person's salary on his/her departure?

Tough

- Why did the candidate leave the job?
- Could I read you the part of the candidate's resume that describes the work that he/she did for your organization, and could you comment on the accuracy of this information?
- How reliable is the candidate? How honest is he/she?
- How does the candidate compare to the person who is currently doing the job?
- Can you think of any specific situation in which he/she did something extraordinary?
- What would you say are the candidate's strengths? Shortcomings?
- Would you hire this person again for the same job?

BE WARY OF DISCRIMINATORY QUESTIONS DURING REFERENCE CHECKS

DANGER!

Even though it may not seem so on the surface, conversations with references are bound by the same legal constraints that govern the content of interview questions. In short, any question that has to do with a candidate's age, gender, marital status, race, ethnic background, or physical condition is out of bounds and could boomerang into a lawsuit. Questions to references should deal only with job-specific issues.

Stellar Performer: David Blumenthal Turning the Tables

David Blumenthal, president and owner of a New Jersey-based information/technology consulting company called Flash Creative Management, has an unusual way of dealing with the reference-checking aspect of hiring, according to a 1995 article published in *HR Magazine*. Whenever he's interviewing a candidate who shows promise, Blumenthal hands a list of names and phone numbers to the applicant and instructs him or her to give the people a call and ask them about his company. The references happen to be clients with whom Blumenthal has dealt for years. They are familiar with Blumenthal's technique and apparently do not mind being part of this process. After the candidate has had a chance to call these "references," Blumenthal gets in touch with them to find out how the candidate handled himself or herself over the phone. The questions he asks include, "Did the applicant seem genuinely interested in the company?" Blumenthal, according to *HR Magazine*, swears by the technique. He calls it the "foundation" of his hiring practices.[6]

SIMPLE MEASURES

There are a handful of simple, noninvasive steps in reference checking that can be handled by just about anybody in the company but could nonetheless turn up inconsistencies that warrant further investigation. These include the following.

- Verifying the candidate's address and phone number in the local phone directory (if there are inconsistencies, ask about them).
- Checking superior courts for criminal convictions and civil courts for civil judgements.
- Sending a self-addressed form letter to educational institutions listed in the candidate's resume to verify credentials.
- Sending similar letters to any professional associations the candidate has listed.
- Visiting the Internet—the candidate may have a Web site. You may also be able to verify credentials and other information by viewing public records on-line.

HOW TO HANDLE RELUCTANT CANDIDATES

To what lengths should a company go to woo candidates who (1) aren't sure whether they really want the job being offered or (2) are being pursued by other companies?

There are two general schools of thought on this. John Drake, in *Interviewing for Managers,* argues that the ability to "market the job" is as important a part of the selection procedure as recruiting and evaluating candidates.[7] Other hiring specialists, however, see a danger in pushing too hard to rope in a candidate who is having reservations about accepting the offer. "There is a fine line between an offer that is attractive and an offer that is *too* attractive," says Marc Schiller, a New York-based consultant with Price Waterhouse who has specialized in the past in helping small companies develop and work through expansion plans. By "too attractive," Schiller means an offer that makes it so easy for the candidate that the incentive to perform gets compromised. "There is always a temptation, when you are negotiating with a candidate that you really want badly," he says, "to sweeten the deal so much that you remove what might very well be the most attractive aspect of the job: the challenge."[8]

Two issues, above all, should be kept foremost in mind whenever a candidate is having trouble making up his or her mind about the offer. The first has to do with how good the candidate really is—or, to put it another way, how much the company is likely to suffer if the candidate eventually says no. If the company has other options (i.e., other candidates who look as though they could handle the job), the leverage in any negotiations between the company and candidate rests with the company. The second issue is whether the candidate who is wavering is having trouble articulating the source of the ambivalence (see Table 8.3). When the candidate has the leverage, though, the key is to find out where the resistance originates and focus on those areas during subsequent negotiations.

When faced with a reluctant candidate, give special consideration to market conditions, specif-

TABLE 8.3 WHY CANDIDATES HESITATE

Any hesitation a candidate feels about accepting a job offer is almost always a function of one or more of the following factors. Once these issues are brought to the surface, companies are in a better position to know which areas of resistance can be overcome and which may be insurmountable.

- The nature and specifics of the job
- Opportunity for career advancement
- Base salary and frequency of salary review
- Quality of the benefits package (especially when compared to the package offered in the previous job)
- The culture and working style of the company
- Family-friendly policies (opportunities for flextime, child care assistance, etc.)
- The length (and ease) of the commute
- The personality of the person to whom the candidate will report
- Opportunities for self-development (i.e., policy on tuition assistance)
- Impact on family if relocation is necessary
- Perceived solvency of the company

ically how difficult it is to find qualified candidates. It could be that offering a little more than the going rate for the position may be enough to convince the candidate to come on board. If the candidate is still not persuaded, consider alternative perquisites such as flextime, telecommuting, or additional time off to supplement base salary. In addition, performance-based pay such as bonuses is gaining popularity with employers and employees alike as an immediate reward for outstanding achievements. This incentive, results-oriented compensation method gives employees the opportunity to significantly impact their pay. Some other bargaining tools to consider are a performance review with a raise opportunity after six months, a signing bonus, or relocation expense reimbursement.

Candidates that are still undecided at this point may be struggling with compatibility issues. They may doubt their own ability to perform the job required, or even their desire to have the job at all. In this case, some serious questions should be posed to the candidate to get at the root of his or her reluctance. Trying to force a fit with a reticent candidate will be costly to both of you in the end.

THE GROWING IMPORTANCE OF EMPLOYMENT CONTRACTS

Writing in the January 1997 issue of *Management Review,* Lee E. Miller noted that when he first started at Macy's in 1984, no one in the company had an employment contract, but by the time he left 10 years later, "almost no senior executives would agree to join the company unless they were given an employment contract."[9] In a 1995 survey by Robert Half International, 30 percent of executives polled stated that they were using employment contracts more frequently.

Employment contracts spell out such terms of employment as compensation, title, and the conditions under which the relationship can be terminated. They may range in length from a one-page letter to scores of pages, depending on the level of the position. The sticking point in such agreements is often the termination clause—more specifically, the severance that will be paid in the event the arrangement doesn't work out. Severance is a major issue in two situations in particular: (1) when the candidate is leaving what he or she perceives to be a secure job; and (2) when accepting the offered job will require the candidate to relocate.

Probably the most important thing to do when presenting an employment contract is to make sure that it has been written or reviewed by legal counsel before it is presented to the candidate. Among other things, attorneys are in a better position than anyone else to differentiate those aspects of the agreement that are enforceable and those that aren't.

END POINT

Getting reliable reference information about candidates who are under serious consideration for employment has always been a vital component of the hiring process. With the fear of retaliatory suits from disgruntled ex-employees running higher than ever, however, the challenge of obtaining candid information has taken on a new dimension. Although recent legislation in more than 20 states now provides protection for companies that communicate "good-faith" reference information, most large companies still have tight-lipped policies when it comes to issuing a reference. Consequently, companies in need of reference information must be not only persistent in their efforts but resourceful and inventive as well. A growing trend in reference checking today is the use of outside reference-gathering services, but companies who use these services need to remember that if the consultants violate invasion of privacy or discrimination laws in their investigative efforts, the companies who've hired them may be held liable.

These difficulties notwithstanding, there are a number of steps a company can take to overcome the obstacles. These include making reference verification a precondition of hiring and asking the candidate probing questions about job-related skills, experience, and qualifications. Once a candidate's references have been checked, the only remaining obstacle is reaching final agreement with the candidate on the terms of employment. If the candidate is eager to start, this phase of hiring should go relatively smoothly, but if he or she is having second thoughts or is being wooed by another company, the company doing the hiring has to decide how hard it wants to push to bring the candidate into the fold. The negotiation process will usually work to everyone's advantage if the candidate and the company can bring to the surface all the issues that underlie the decision.

MORE READING

Barada, Paul W. "Reference Checking is More Important Than Ever. Reviewing and Providing Job References." *HR Magazine* (November 1996, vol. 41, no. 11), p. 49 (3).

Carvell, Tim. "It's a Seller's Market for Nerds." *Fortune Magazine* (December 9, 1996, vol. 134, no. 11), p. 31 (2).

Caudron, Shari. "Reference Checking Gets Creative. Survival Guide for Recruitment in the '90s." *Workforce* magazine, formerly known as *Personnel Journal* (August 1994, vol. 73, no. 8), p. S22 (2).

Fenn, Donna. "Reference-Checking Woes. Human Resource Executives Report Being Misinformed on a Wide Range of Topics by Inadequate Job References." *Inc.* (December 1995, vol. 17, no. 18), p. 120 (1).

Fisher, Anne. "Is My Paycheck Too Paltry? . . . Will I Like Corporate Life? . . . and Other Queries." *Fortune Magazine* (June 9, 1997, vol. 135, no. 11), p. 165 (2).

King, Julia. "They'll Do Anything to Lure Tech Talent." *Computerworld* (January 20, 1997, vol. 31, no. 3), p. 67 (2).

Laabs, Jennifer J. "Embrace Today's New Deal: Mutual Responsibility between Employer and Employee." *Workforce* magazine, formerly known as *Personnel Journal* (August 1996, vol. 75, no. 8), p. 60 (4).

Lewis, Victoria V. "Hirings, Firings Can Make or Break an Agency." *National Underwriter Property & Casualty-Risk & Benefits Management* (October 21, 1996, no. 43), p. 13 (3).

Petras, Kathryn and Ross Petras. "How to Turn a Job Offer into a Plum Deal." *Executive Female* (September/October 1993, vol. 16, no. 5), p. 31 (7).

Phaneuf, Anne M. "Bartering for Benefits: When a Job Offer Falls Short on Dollars, Negotiate for Nonsalary Benefits." *Sales & Marketing Management* (December 1995, vol. 147, no. 12), p. 82 (2).

Robinson, Sandra L. "Trust and Breach of the Psychological Contract." *Administrative Science Quarterly* (December 1996, vol. 41, no. 4), p. 574 (26).

Turner, Dan. "Disney's Go-Go Growth Days May Be Going, Going, Gone." *Los Angeles Business Journal* (March 3, 1997, vol. 19, no. 9), p. 1 (2).

Winans, Brent and Gregory Cairns. "Background Checking: Reducing Workers' Compensation Claims. How to Legally Screen Employment Applicants Who Pose Fraud, Reinjury Risks." *Risk Management* (October 1996, vol. 43, no. 10), p. 31 (5).

CHAPTER

Retaining and Getting the Most out of High-Performing Employees

INTRODUCTION

It isn't only their ability to recruit and hire outstanding candidates that separates companies that are thriving in today's marketplace from the rest. No less important is their ability to tap the full potential of candidates once they've been hired. Meeting the latter of these two challenges has always been a critical priority in business, but in today's environment the challenge of keeping good employees motivated and committed has become greatly magnified. This chapter looks at three of the key aspects of this challenge: (1) orientation; (2) training; and (3) quality of work-life policies.

HUMAN RESOURCES MANAGEMENT PRACTICES AND THE BOTTOM LINE

There is a great deal of anecdotal evidence and theoretical research to support the notion that certain human resources management practices can have a direct and positive impact on such strategic priorities as productivity, turnover, and financial performance. Empirical studies that shed some light on these connections, however, are few and far between. One notable exception is a study conducted in the early 1990s by Dr.

Mark A. Huselid, an assistant professor at the School of Management and Labor Relations at Rutgers University. Huselid's research specialty is finding linkages between human resource management systems, corporate strategy, and company performance.

Dr. Huselid's methodology was as follows. He identified seven different human resource management (HRM) practices and then developed a survey designed to determine how prevalent these practices were in companies throughout the United States. He then compared the results of the survey with publicly available financial and productivity data on each company. Among the key HRM practices that were the basis of the study were the following.

- A formal information-sharing program (a newsletter, for instance)
- A formal job analysis process that identifies core competencies needed for each position
- Attitude surveys conducted on a regular basis among employees
- Level of employee participation (quality circles, for example)
- Employee access to incentive plans and profit sharing
- Formal performance appraisals
- Training

Dr. Huselid obtained survey results from nearly 1000 companies—25 percent of the companies to which surveys were sent—and used a variety of complex financial and mathematical models to develop his thesis. He was careful to concede in the report he published that his methodology had its limitations, particularly when it came to relating HRM practices to short- and long-term measures of corporate financial performance. He also pointed out that his turnover data did not make a distinction between voluntary and involuntary turnover. Generally, though, the results he obtained offer empirical evidence that companies employing the seven HRM practices do indeed experience less turnover, more productivity, and better financial performance than companies that don't employ such practices.

Huselid reports, for instance, that there was a 40 percent difference in turnover rate between companies whose use of HRM practices placed them three points *above* the mean (when Huselid scored the survey results) and companies whose survey results placed them three points *below* the mean. This meant that there was a tremendous difference in turnover rates between companies whose scores were only six points apart on the rating scale.

Dr. Huselid suggested, too, on the basis of his findings, that investments in HRM practices could increase both cash flow and market value, although he cautions that the ROI has to analyzed on a reasonably long-term basis.

Although it is difficult for the average businessperson to fully grasp the technical aspects of Dr. Huselid's study, his findings, along with his sophisticated methodology, are likely to spark research that will document the bottom-line implications of savvy human resource management practices.[1]

ORIENTATION: MAKING SURE EMPLOYEES GET OFF ON THE RIGHT FOOT

Employee orientation has long been one of those business practices that companies take for granted. In the vast majority of businesses there is no formal orientation process. Instead, the newly hired employee gets a quick run-through of the office or plant environment, conducted by whoever happens to be around. Even in companies that have structured programs, the process tends to be routine and uninspired. New employees are typically assembled for a series of oral presentations (and occasionally a video) and given handouts that offer some background on the company and explain basic policies and benefits.

Attitudes are changing. There is more recognition that even the most talented and skilled new employees need more time and guidance to acclimate themselves to new environments, new people, and new responsibilities. And there is considerable evidence to suggest that what happens during the first few days of a new employee's work experience has more bearing than previously thought on such long-term factors as productivity, relationships with coworkers, job satisfaction, and turnover.

Examples of innovative orientation practices can now be found in a growing number of progressive companies, with much of the new thinking on orientation inspired by the Walt Disney Company, whose orientation programs are often used by companies seeking to revamp their policies. At Disney, the key element to a successful orientation program is emotion—creating excitement for the Disney culture. The two-day initial training session attended by all new Disney "cast members" at the Walt Disney World Resort in Buena Vista, for example, was once described by *Fortune* as "part inculcation, part encounter group." Disney, however, makes no apologies. Indeed, one of the stated goals of its orientation is to give new employees a clear understanding of how the company works and what it takes to get along in Disney's "corporate family."[2]

Another major hospitality company that believes fervently in the power of effectively run orientation programs is the Marriott Corporation. As *Fortune* reported, Marriott decided to revisit its orientation policies at the same time it was overhauling its recruiting policies—all part of a companywide campaign to reduce the turnover rate among newly hired front-line employees. A more systematic approach to recruiting helped to lower that rate, but Richard Bell-Irving, Marriott's vice president of lodging human resources, gives much of the credit for the increased retention to the company's new approach toward orientation.

What the company used to do, Bell-Irving told *Fortune,* was hire new associates, tell them about benefit plans, then put the employees out in front of the customers and instruct them to "go for it." But that's all changed. Marriott's new employee orientation functions as a combination orientation, training, and probation period. It begins with an eight-hour session, the highlight of which is an "elegant lunch" served by veteran hotel employees. After that first session, each new associate is assigned a mentor, known as a "buddy." New employees attend refresher courses after the first and second months. After 90 days, the hotel treats the entire class to a banquet.[3]

While it takes money, resources, and time to emulate the orientation practices of Disney and Marriott, senior officials at both companies are convinced that the investment more than pays for itself in enhanced productivity and reduced turnover. See Table 9.1 for hints on developing your own orientation program.

TABLE 9.1 FIVE KEYS TO STARTING AN ORIENTATION PROGRAM FROM SCRATCH

Get feedback from current employees. The best way to determine what issues should be addressed and what topics should be covered in an orientation program is to talk to employees and find out directly what information *they* think should be included. When preparing an orientation program for its maintenance division, for instance, the University of Minnesota assembled a focus group of 29 randomly selected employees, all of whom had been hired within the previous six months to a year.[4]

Communicate the big picture. Don't underestimate the importance of providing employees at all levels with an overview of what the company does and what makes it unique. Employees should be introduced to as many different aspects of the business as possible, even though they may not be directly involved with a particular department. Only then will they be able to understand how their jobs fit into the overall system. National Semiconductor, for instance, begins its half-day orientation program by introducing new employees to the semiconductor industry as a whole. It then shows a video that provides an overview of the corporate identity. The first day also includes "window tours" that give employees an opportunity to see the products and production processes firsthand.[5]

Put key information in written form. The documentation that explains employee policies and benefits doesn't have to be glossy or slick, but it should be in written form and should spell out the basic policies clearly and succinctly.

Get current employees involved. The people best qualified to orient new employees are those who are already working for the company and who have a strong sense of the company culture. The more interaction new employees have with current employees, the faster the new employees will adjust to the new culture.

Show some imagination. There are no rules as such for conducting an effective orientation program—no set time frame or structure. Companies should not be afraid to experiment—to create an orientation program that captures the spirit and the mood of the company.

CHANGING TIDES IN ORIENTATION

Although each has its own unique wrinkle, the most effective orientation programs today feature many of the same basic practices that distinguish the programs at Disney and Marriott. For one thing, successful orientation activities tend to focus as much on culture as they do on policies and procedures. For another, they take place over an extended period of time instead of a single day. They usually make use of current employees, who serve as "mentors," "buddies," or "sponsors." In addition, they all tend to combine the transfer of company information with training and indoctrination into the company culture.

A case in point is Micron Technology, a chip maker based in Boise, Idaho.[6] Like most successful, fast-growing high-tech companies, Micron Technology never took the time in its formative years to develop a structured approach to orientation. It relied instead on a practice commonly known throughout the company as "instant immersion." Micron employees were left to their own devices when it came to learning how to adapt to the company. But as the size of its workforce began to mushroom—the employee population more than doubled between the 1980s and early 1990s—Micron, according to a report published in *Training and Development* in 1993, found itself with a problem common to many of its counterparts in the computer industry: It was taking longer and longer for new employees to acclimate themselves to Micron's fast-paced, team-oriented culture. Employee surveys revealed that most new employees felt "overwhelmed and confused." Very few understood the link between their jobs and the whole of Micron's operation. Many were frustrated by what they perceived to be a lack of opportunity.

To its credit, Micron met the problem head-on. Rather than placing the blame on the new employees for their failure to meet Micron standards, the company pulled together an internal team and vested it with the responsibility of developing an orientation program that would address the problems the surveys had uncovered. The team met regularly for three months, and with the help of feedback from managers throughout the company, it created a program it now calls Reaching High Performance (RHP).

RHP takes 15 hours and is administered in seven sessions (each running for 2 hours) spread across six weeks. Each RHP unit brings together about 30 new employees and is generally run by a facilitator as well as a cofacilitator who is a manager from one of the company's various departments. The program begins with a big-picture view of Micron's history and mission and, as it unfolds, becomes increasingly more application oriented, with many of the classroom exercises designed to enhance the ability of trainees to work together in teams.

A typical activity is a simulation exercise in which one of the new employees is chosen as the "supervisor of the day." The supervisor is given the job of creating a product (an object made of folded origami paper) and then trains other members of the team to make the product. The supervisor has to create a set of written specifications and then make sure the product is properly designed before being delivered to the customer. RHP has been modified slightly over the years, but the program has been running strong since its inception, and it continues today.

Another example of an innovative, multitiered, culture-driven approach to orientation is one developed in the early 1990s by DuPont Merck Pharmaceutical Company.[7] As at Micron Technology, the orientation is viewed as a process, not simply an introductory meeting. The orientation takes place over time and is keyed as much to issues involving values and culture as to policies and procedures.

The program is divided into three stages, or *tiers,* with each tier keyed to a different objective. The first tier is held shortly after the employee is hired and focuses on big-picture topics: culture and values. The second phase, which takes place anywhere from 30 to 90 days after the employee's first day, is designed to help employees see the relationship between corporate goals and what they do as individuals. The final phase usually takes place one to two months later, and gives employees the opportunity to "look at company goals within the context of divisional activities."

One of the key features of DuPont's program is the emphasis on "teaming." During the first session, which takes place shortly after the employee is hired, each new hire becomes a part of an "orienteering" team that includes his or her supervisor, a sponsor, and an administrative coordinator.

The overall goal of this program, according to Bill DeLorbe, vice president of human resources for DuPont Merck Pharmaceutical, is to "thoroughly indoctrinate the new employee in the Merck-DuPont culture. We're creating an environment that is built on quality, diversity and performance that allows us to recruit, motivate, retain and recognize our people. That's the key to our success."

See Table 9.2 for features an orientation program should provide.

TABLE 9.2 DON'T FORGET THE BASICS

In all cases, an orientation program should provide new employees with the basic information they need to operate comfortably and effectively in their new environment. Here's a brief checklist of the key considerations.

- An overview of the company—how big it is, what it sells, and how long it's been in business.
- Location of facilities—restrooms, eating places, photocopy room, and other areas.
- Work hours, including breaks and lunch hours.
- Basic compensation policies and benefits. Especially important: making sure that somebody familiar with the process (ideally a human resources representative) provides an orientation on benefits and explains how and when paychecks are distributed.
- Health and safety considerations, such as fire escapes, exits, and first aid kits.
- Information about the phone system and other office equipment.
- Who to call in case of problems or difficulties.
- Employee reward and incentive programs.[8]

EVERYTHING COUNTS MORE AT FIRST

A study published in 1996 in the *Cornell Hotel & Restaurant Administration Quarterly* strongly illustrates that new employees are highly impressionable during the first few days on the job and can often form strong attitudes (both positive and negative) on the basis of a single incident. One of the respondents in the study reported, for instance, how impressed he was by the culture of "family" that prevailed in one of the companies he worked for early in his career. But this attitude wasn't shaped by anything the respondent had read in the company's mission statement or heard during its orientation session. The impression was forged when the company's CEO offered to lend the respondent his car until the respondent could buy his own car.

Another respondent reported, by contrast, that after two meetings with her program coordinator, she was convinced that the coordinator cared little about her or her career progress. The reason: The coordinator asked the same questions in both sessions. According to the respondent, "It made me feel as though she was meeting with me because it was her duty—and not because she cared about my progress."[9]

PICK MENTORS AND SPONSORS WITH CARE

One of the more common features of today's best orientation programs is a "buddy" or "mentor" system in which each new employee is paired with a current employee who knows the ropes and helps to shepherd the new employee through the early days of employment. Obviously, that person needs to be chosen with care, and in this regard, the University of Minnesota has established some useful criteria.[10] Employees who help new university hires become more oriented to the culture are (1) relatively new to the job themselves (from six months to a year); (2) already performing well on the job; and (3) judged to be team players.

ORIENTATION: THE SUPERVISOR'S ROLE

Whether the orientation is conducted formally or informally, the new employee's manager should always play a key role in the process. Here are some guidelines for managers to follow when they are about to bring a new employee on board.

- Be on hand personally (if possible) to introduce the new employee to coworkers.
- Sit down with the employee and discuss the job, its relationship to other jobs in the department, the department's mission, and the standards by which the employee's work will be evaluated.
- Make sure that the new employee's work area is equipped with necessary supplies and equipment.
- Have one or two specific assignments that will enable the new employee to be productive immediately and create an early sense of accomplishment.
- Choose mentors, sponsors, or buddies with care, making sure that whoever is chosen wants to do the job and has a positive attitude toward the company.
- Discuss whatever special training the employee will be expected to participate in and why the training is required.
- Visit with the new hire at the end of the day to see how things are going and to determine whether there is a need for additional information.
- Monitor the employee's performance over the first few months. Even if the company doesn't have a formal probation period, the employee should be told what constitutes reasonable job progress. Both good and unsatisfactory work should be mentioned.
- Use this time to learn from the employee new ways in which the work could be done. Be open-minded to the employee's ideas.[11]

THE NEW EMPLOYMENT CONTRACT

Although its terms are rarely set to paper, there now exists in many companies what some people have chosen to call the "new employment deal"—the implicit understanding between employer and employee in high-performance companies. Here's how Marc Effron, director of organization effectiveness for Oxford Health Plans, in Norwalk, Connecticut, explained the concept to Jennifer Laabs in the August 1996 issue of *Workforce* magazine:

> *"We define the 'new employment deal' as an even exchange of performance and assumed risk for rewards. You're expected to work at a torrid pace and focus all your facilities on producing timely, creative, sound business results that are in the best interests of the member, provider, shareholder and community. In exchange, you're provided with unbelievably large opportunities to prove yourself in a fast-growing field and with a premier company and the rewards that go with it."*[12]

In her exploration of this new concept, Laabs focused in particular on skills development as the primary driver in the process. "What savvy employees are after these days," she says, "are portable or transferable skills, and a variety of cross-functional assignments. This is what employers have to deliver under the new deal."

TRAINING AND DEVELOPMENT IN THE NEW WORKPLACE

Training has always been a fundamental part of the work experience. Few would dispute that regardless of how skilled, talented, or knowledgeable employees may be, there will always be aspects of their job performance that could benefit from proper training and skills development. Business research literature is rich with studies showing clearly that certain types of training can have a dramatically positive impact on productivity, safety, job performance, employee morale, and job satisfaction. And there is widespread acknowledgment among business leaders throughout the United States that companies have little choice but to invest more time, effort, and money into the development of their work forces.

While nobody would disparage the importance of education and training in today's workplace, the track record of corporate training in America, by most accounts, is nothing to brag about. True, American companies currently spend in excess of $30 billion a year on training, but 90 percent of that total, according to the American Society of Training and Development, is spent by fewer than 1 percent of all the companies in the United States. And the vast majority of this money is spent on a relatively small proportion of the labor force—less than 10 percent.[13] Still, more and more companies today, mainly by necessity, have begun to view training in a different light. Here's a brief overview of the state of corporate training today, as we approach the year 2000.

- A combination of familiar factors—new technologies, fewer middle managers to supervise, and increasing emphasis on customer service as a competitive weapon—has created the need for millions of front-line employees to develop new competencies, particularly those involving interpersonal skills. The need is especially acute among service industries, where a lack of strong interpersonal skills can have a direct impact on customer satisfaction and sales.
- An increasingly high percentage of entry-level workers—including those who have college degrees—are lacking in the basic skills (reading, writing, math, etc.) that constitute the building blocks of the training they will require to keep pace with the mushrooming growth of technology in the workplace.
- Decisions regarding who receives training have become increasingly decentralized, with line managers controlling budgets and making decisions that were previously under the control of

corporate training departments. The role of the training department in many companies is no longer to organize a curriculum but to work with line managers to choose which programs meet business goals.

- A small but growing number of major companies—General Electric, for instance—have committed themselves to a value generally known as *lifelong learning.* The premise, simply put, is that the only way companies can hope to keep pace with the technology and competitive pressures is to make training and development an ongoing process.[14]
- More companies than ever are insisting that training be tied to strategic business goals, but the yardstick by which training is measured is expanding, with more factors being taken into account when the impact of training is being evaluated. Frederick Reichheld argues in *The Loyalty Effect* that "loyalty leaders" must invest heavily in the development and training of their employees, not simply to enhance performance but to enhance a company's ability to retain its customers. "As employees stay on," notes Reichheld, "they get better at their jobs and become better acquainted with their customers; employee loyalty and customer loyalty reinforce each other."[15]
- Delivery methods for training in companies have begun to change dramatically. With the availability of advanced technology and more people working flexible hours and from home, it is becoming more complicated and more expensive for companies to conduct training in formal classrooms. A small but rapidly growing number of companies have begun to provide training that originates from the Internet and through their own Intranets. And the number of computer-based training products is rising almost daily. This new form of training is sometimes referred to as *computer-based* or *distance* training. The idea, in any event, is the same: To provide training in a way that doesn't oblige employees to travel to a training site and that

gives them almost unlimited flexibility when it comes to setting up their own training sessions.

HOW TO CHOOSE THE RIGHT TRAINING

Training decisions are complex. Delivery options abound, and the price range for programs that teach the same general set of competencies (time management, for instance) can range from less than $50 for a do-it-yourself audio course to as high as $5000 or more for one of the growing number of executive education programs offered by faculty members at institutions such as the Wharton School of Business at the University of Pennsylvania and the Darden School of Business Administration at the University of Virginia.

Unfortunately, there is no way to measure the relative value of these programs. There are too many variables, and too much of the learning process depends on the motivation level of the person being trained. Nonetheless, there are some basic questions that should always serve as the foundation of training decisions in general. These follow, along with suggestions on how to determine answers (also see Table 9.3).

TABLE 9.3 TRAINING DO'S

- Tie the training to business goals.
- Conduct rigorous needs assessment to determine what competencies are required and what gap exists between current competency levels and skills required.
- Involve the employees who will undergo the training in the process and convey the importance of the training and its relevance to their careers.
- Choose the training source carefully: Don't be driven by economics alone.
- If at all possible, conduct the training during work hours instead of at night or on the weekends. (Otherwise, employees will sometimes view the time they spend as a sacrifice rather than an opportunity to learn.)
- Conduct the training in a facility that's comfortable and where the environment sends a positive message.
- Give thought to how the impact of the training is to be measured.

What Business Need Will the Training Serve?

Action required: A thorough analysis of the business, designed to identify the competencies necessary to meet strategic objectives.

Who Should Receive the Training?

Action required: A needs assessment that can uncover gaps between the competencies required to meet strategic objectives and the current skills employees possess.

What Form Should the Training Take?

Action required: Market research (reading, networking, and visits to conventions). Look into all the possibilities, with budget considerations always kept in mind.

Which Training Vendors Should Be Chosen?

Action required: As much research as possible into what makes one vendor different from others, what the firm offers, the cost, and what has been accomplished for key clients.

How Should the Training Be Scheduled?

Action required: Communication with employees and supervisors to determine which schedule is likely to accomplish the training objectives—without creating unacceptable levels of disruption in the department.

How Can the Effects of Training Be Measured?

Action required: Establishing expectations and setting up a process that can measure the long-term impact.

HOW TO TELL WHETHER TRAINING WORKS

The benefits of training are particularly difficult to measure: As mentioned earlier, there are simply

Stellar Performer: **Motorola, Inc.**

It would be difficult to name any company in the United States that has demonstrated a stronger commitment to the ongoing training and education of its employees than Motorola, Inc.[16] Motorola reportedly spends upward of $120 million yearly on training, most of it conducted in its 133,000-square foot Motorola University, which is located at the company's headquarters in Schaumburg, Illinois. The company also has 14 other branches of the university throughout the United States, Europe, Asia, and Latin America.

Training at Motorola isn't an option: it's a requirement. All Motorola employees must attend at least five days of training every year. The company's training function employs more than 1200 specialists, including 110 who work full-time as classroom trainers. The curriculum at Motorola University includes periodic classes that last half a day to two weeks and cover such topics as quality, risk-taking, managing change, basic skills courses in reading and math, and teamwork. Each of the functional classes—engineering, manufacturing, and sales and marketing—is divided into three parts: relational skills (such as customer satisfaction, effective supervision, negotiation, and persuasive presentations), technical skills, and business skills.

Most of Motorola's courses have been internally developed and make liberal use of state-of-the-art learning techniques. When factory workers are learning the fundamentals of computer-aided design, for instance, they not only attend lectures and read manuals, they also create their own plastic models of actual products. Noteworthy, too, is that most of the people who conduct the training are not professional trainers. Many are employees who have a knack for teaching.

Although Motorola has no formal measuring process for the impact of its training, the company estimates that for every dollar it spends on training, it gets back some $30 in productivity gains within three years. The company reports that since 1987 it has been able to cut its costs by $3.3 billion—not by eliminating personnel but by "training them to simplify processes and reduce waste. Sales per employee have doubled in the past five years, and profits have increased 47 percent."

too many variables that can affect the outcome. What's more, it is impossible to separate the direct benefits (i.e., what is actually learned in the courses) from the indirect benefits (i.e., the added motivation and morale boost) people derive from going through the process.

The most commonly used system of evaluating training is based on a four-tier model developed in 1958 by a University of Wisconsin professor named Donald Kirkpatrick. Often referred to as "the Kirkpatrick model," the analysis is based on four criteria.[17]

- *Employee reaction:* The satisfaction level of trainees as expressed in post-training evaluation forms (see Table 9.4 for suggestions on the content of these forms).
- *Learning:* The extent to which a trainee's skills or knowledge have grown as the result of the training. Learning is easier to measure in training programs that focus on hard skills versus "people skills."
- *Behavioral change:* The impact of the training on job performance.
- *Results:* The impact of the training on company operations.

TABLE 9.4 GETTING FEEDBACK—POST-TRAINING SURVEYS

The following questions can serve as the basis of a post-training survey of participants who've completed a program.

- Did the program meet your expectations?
- Did the material covered in the seminar relate directly to your job responsibilities?
- How knowledgeable was the instructor?
- How sensitive to the needs of the audience was the instructor?
- Would you recommend the program to other employees?
- How was the quality of the workbook materials?
- Was the length of the program appropriate?

Source: Business Week, *September 16, 1996, by permission of* Business Week *© 1997.*

CREATING A FAMILY-FRIENDLY WORK ENVIRONMENT

Quality of life has become one of the most significant business issues in the 1990s—so much so that the topic has been the subject of cover stories in several major national magazines, including *U.S. News and World Report* and *Business Week.* The theme underlying each of these cover stories has been the same. Demographic changes in the workplace—and, in particular, the influx of working mothers—coupled with the push for higher performance brought on by globalization, have created pressures on employees that companies can no longer ignore. As Amy Saltzman pointed out in *U.S. News and World Report,* "Most companies now realize that they must make concessions to a world where both parents work."[18] And Keith Hammonds, writing in *Business Week,* added: "Work-family strategies haven't just hit the corporate mainstream—they've become a competitive advantage."[19]

Both reports, along with the dozens of other articles that have been written about this subject over the past several years, are rich with examples of companies that have taken specific measures to help their employees do a better job of juggling the pressures of the job with the pressures from home (see Table 9.5). The message that comes through loud and clear in all these reports is that the solution involves more than simply implementing family-friendly policies such as telecommuting, flextime, and child care assistance. Ultimately required are fundamental changes in culture and lifestyle. As Saltzman explained it, "Rather than appending 'family friendly' programs to a traditional conception of office life, firms are redefining the nature of work itself, making balanced lives for employees a central tenet around which the rest of the company is designed."[20]

The specific steps that companies are taking to make life easier for their employees vary considerably from one company to the next, but the one

TABLE 9.5 REPORTS FROM THE FIELD: EXAMPLES OF HOW COMPANIES BALANCE WORK AND FAMILY, AS CITED IN RECENT ARTICLES

- Motorola issues pagers to expectant fathers during the final trimesters of their wives' pregnancies.[21]
- Eddie Bauer keeps its headquarters café open late so that it can prepare takeout for employees who work overtime.[22]
- Hewlett-Packard requires that every business unit identify work-family issues and propose an action plan as part of its annual business review. So when HP's printer group, facing higher consumer demand, had to increase the number of shifts its manufacturing employees worked, it also investigated alternatives for round-the-clock child care.[23]
- IBM gives seed and equipment money to local child care agencies to assist them with opening child care centers near IBM offices.[24]
- Andersen Consulting offers a "concierge" service in several of its offices throughout the United States. The service makes available to Andersen consultants people who can do many of the personal errands—driving a car to the local service center, for instance—that would otherwise cut into office time.[25]
- United HealthCare joined with Connecticut-based Dependent Care Connection to provide dependent care counseling, education, and referral services as part of its OPTUM CARE24, a 24-hour, toll-free information line that helps employees cope with any health- or well-being-related concern.[26]

common denominator is flexibility—management's willingness to experiment with work practices that would have been unheard-of as recently as 20 years ago.

Companies are focusing less on policies and more on the reorganization of work. Employers getting the best results from their family-friendly policies, as a general rule, have transferred responsibility for determining how and when work gets done from management to the people who actually do the jobs. This transfer, of course, doesn't work in every industry and doesn't lend itself to every company, but it has met with notable success in companies that have already committed themselves to a team-oriented, self-directed culture. *Business Week* reported, for instance, that when workers at General Motors'

Saturn Co. were given a chance to plan their own schedules, the result was something quite unlike the typical work week in the automotive industry. Employees decided to set up a four-day, 10-hour-a-day work week, with rotating day and night shifts—an arrangement that gave workers more options than the normal work week and also enabled the company to keep the plant operating six days a week, 20 hours a day, with minimal overtime. At the end of each three-week rotation, workers get five consecutive days off. Because they don't need to use leave time for appointments, these employees have fewer personal obligations that cut into productivity. And because teams are responsible for deciding how management's goals will be met, employees who need a day off can simply switch with another team member when personal problems do arise.[27]

Family-friendly policies clearly go a long way to ease the pressure on employees and, by doing so, enhance employee satisfaction. But how these policies ultimately affect a company's bottom line is another question. No one to date has produced any major, long-term study that demonstrates definitive connections between specific family-friendly policies and productivity, but there are a handful of small-scale studies and a great deal of anecdotal evidence to indicate that a correlation does exist.

After extending its unpaid parental leave to six months, Aetna Life & Casualty halved the rate of resignations among new mothers, saving $1 million a year in hiring and training expenses. When researchers at the University of Chicago surveyed employees at Fel-Pro, a Skokie, Illinois–based automotive products company that had instituted a wide range of family-friendly policies, it found that nearly all the measures of productivity and job satisfaction improved. Quality improvement suggestions, for instance, doubled. And supervisors reported that employees who had been given more autonomy in their jobs not only were less stressed but also were much more committed to their work.[28]

GOODBYE TO "9 TO 5"

Virtually all survey data published on work-life issues has underscored what most employees have been witnessing or experiencing for themselves: a dramatic increase in the number of working arrangements that depart from the "9 to 5" tradition (see Table 9.6). For instance, a 1997 survey developed by Robert Half International revealed the following results on two key aspects of this trend: flexible hours and telecommuting. The responses were drawn from a pool of 150 executives from the nation's 1000 largest companies.

Percentage of Respondents Whose Firms

- Currently offer an informal flexible hours program: 47
- Currently offer a formalized flexible hours program: 37
- Offer neither: 12

Percentage of Respondents Who Believe That in the Next Five Years the Number of Employees in Their Companies Telecommuting Will

- Increase strongly: 35
- Increase somewhat: 52
- Not change: 9
- Decrease somewhat: 4

Clearly, technology has been a key catalyst for this change. Wide-area networks, wireless communication, and the Internet are making it increasingly

TABLE 9.6 TELECOMMUTING EMPLOYEES

The number of employees who telecommute (officially accepted definition: work at home at least one day per month during normal business hours) is clearly on the rise. A survey conducted in the mid-1990s by *American Information User* shows the total may be as high as 11 million.[29] The survey also states, however, that the vast majority of telecommuting arrangements are part-time, with telecommuters working on average about 39.6 hours per month.

possible for employees to stay in close touch with their offices even when they're traveling, working flexible hours, or telecommuting.

First Tennessee Bank's CEO, Ralph Horn, conceded to *Business Week* that change didn't occur overnight. As employees began to take more control over the workplace, Horn noted that his managers had to "change the way they did business." Ultimately, the process has proven to be both a social and financial success. Successful supervisors, rated by their subordinates as supportive of work-family balance, retained employees twice as long as the bank average and kept 7 percent more retail customers. Higher retention rates, First Tennessee says, contributed to a 55 percent profit gain over two years, to a total of $106 million overall.[30]

LOYALTY PROGRAMS WORK IN SMALL COMPANIES, TOO

High employee retention can be achieved at small companies. At Donald Dann, a $4 million life insurance sales and marketing firm based in Highland Park, Illinois, roughly half of the 20 employees have been with the company for 15 years or more.[31] How has the company done it? Dann, the founder, shared his "secrets" in an article published in *Nation's Business.*

- A rigorous hiring policy (as many as six interviews before a finalist is chosen) designed to attract self-motivated and self-starting individuals, not those with the most experience.
- An operating philosophy and company culture that gives employees considerable latitude as to how they run their day-to-day jobs, regardless of how long they've been with the company.
- A commitment to training and self-development, manifested in frequent on-site training meetings, encouraging employees to continue their education.
- Frequent salary reviews—every six months rather than annually—to provide more frequent and tangible evidence that the company values the individual's commitment.

Stellar Performer: **First Tennessee Bank**

No major company in the United States, according to *Business Week*, is more family friendly than First Tennessee, an 8000-person bank with branches throughout the South.[33] What sets First Tennessee Bank apart, according to *Business Week*, is not only that it offers luxurious benefits such as on-site child care or vouchers, job sharing, and fitness centers, but that it demonstrates an "intelligent, strategic view of the problem."

First Tennessee reportedly took this tack when it discovered in the early 1990s that those branches that had the greatest customer satisfaction also had the lowest employee turnover. The company decided that to stay competitive it had to take special measures to keep its employees happy. While First Tennessee already had a variety of "family-friendly" programs in place, surveys revealed that few employees took advantage of them. Hence, the bank adopted a new approach that achieved the following.

- Established a new philosophy in which retaining employees took higher priority than profitability
- Created a management training program whose purpose was to link productivity and customer satisfaction to employee satisfaction
- Eliminated many of the work rules, and gave employees the right to decide for themselves how to balance work responsibilities and personal needs

- Positive verbal reinforcement, working to correct problems by going forward rather than dwelling on past mistakes; flextime; birthday and holiday gifts; opportunities for everyone to enjoy incentive plan travel bonuses; and other programs.

"Our company's small size means there are inherent limitations for advancement," Dann admits. "But we encourage employees to tell us what they want from their jobs, and we help them get there—even if that means they eventually will leave our company."[32]

In one of the most ambitious job satisfaction studies of its kind ever conducted, Yuan Ting, associate professor of political science at California State University-Fullerton, analyzed the survey responses of more than 30,000 federal white-collar workers, shedding some interesting light on the subject. Based on Ting's findings, overall job satisfaction is a function of attitudes relating to each of the following aspects of an employee's job.

- Pay levels
- Promotion opportunities
- Task clarity (how clearly procedures and expectations were spelled out to employees)
- Task contribution (understanding by employees of how their jobs contributed to the mission of the agency)
- Relationship with coworkers
- Relationship with supervisors
- Organizational commitment

Ting noted in the discussion of his results that only two of the factors in the list—pay levels and promotion opportunities—are related to money and position. All the others have to do with the quality of the work experience. He suggested, too, that task clarity—making sure that employees have a clear idea of what their roles are and what they are expected to contribute—has a far greater bearing on job satisfaction than many people realize. Further, Ting reminds hiring managers that task clarity is one aspect of the work experience that most companies are in a position to control.[34]

SUCCESS GUIDELINES FOR TELECOMMUTING

The following are four keys to implementing a successful telecommuting policy.

Set an even-handed policy. Before a company sets up individual arrangements with employees who want to telecommute, it should establish a clear set of guidelines that spells out the criteria governing telecommuting arrangements. The absence of such a policy could create resentment among employees who would like to telecommute but are not allowed to participate.

Gear up for it. If telecommuting is going to work, companies may need to be prepared to invest in the equipment that enables telecommuters to stay in touch with their office coworkers. At the very least, a "home office" requires a computer, fax, and some arrangement for e-mail.

Clarify liability issues. Telecommuting arrangements have begun to create confusion in certain areas of personnel management. One issue that needs to be explored and clarified is the workers' compensation status of employees who spend a good portion of their working day at home.

Be prepared to adjust certain work practices. Telecommuting arrangements will not work successfully unless companies are willing to make corresponding changes in the way work is conducted. One big change involves how communication is handled. For example, companies that have traditionally relied on face-to-face meetings have to be willing to handle routine communication by phone or by e-mail.

END POINT

No less important than the ability to recruit and hire top performing employees is the ability to keep them motivated and committed. This chapter addresses three of the most important management practices that have been used successfully by companies in meeting this challenge.

Employee orientations have taken on much more importance now that corporate culture has become a critical factor in productivity and turnover. The trend among many progressive companies today is to combine orientation with training—and to view orientation as an extended program rather than a one-day introduction to the company. Training practices are also changing as companies seek to improve delivery and bring educational goals into better alignment with business goals.

In one of the most significant workplace trends of the 1990s, more companies than ever have begun to introduce policies and procedures that are specifically designed to help employees balance home and work pressures. Quality of life issues have now assumed unprecedented importance among highly-sought-after job candidates, and the ability of a company to address these issues effectively has emerged as a key competitive advantage.

MORE READING

Brewer, Geoffrey. "Seven Secrets to Building Employee Loyalty." *Sales and Marketing Management* (December 1995, vol. 147, no. 12), p. P20(6).

Carson, Kenneth P., Robert L. Cardy, and Gregory H. Dobbins. "Upgrade the Employee Evaluation Process." *HR Magazine* (November 1992, vol. 37, no. 11), p. 88(5).

Clark, Scott. "Find Ways to Build Loyalty, Commitment to Quality." *Puget Sound Business Journal* (December 6, 1996, vol. 17, no. 30), p. 36(1).

Emshoff, James R. "How to Increase Employee Loyalty While You Downsize." *Business Horizons* (March/April 1994, vol. 37, no. 2), p. 49(9).

Kaberline, Brian. "Scott's Dilemma: Union Station's Top Man Ponders Portland Job Offer." *The Kansas City Business Journal* (September 30, 1994, vol. 13, no. 2), p. 3(2).

Kahn, Virginia Munger. "Give This to Your Benefits Person: Companies Are Hiring Outside Firms to

Give Advice to 401(k) Participants." *Financial World* (June 17, 1997, vol. 166, no. 6), p. 93(2).

Levine, Gene. "Proper Orientation Reduces Turnover." *Bobbin* (December 1996, vol. 38, no. 4), p. 70(2).

"Loyalty." *Supervision* (April 1997, vol. 58, no. 4), p. 18(1).

McKendall, Marie and Stephen T. Margulis. "Organizational Loyalty is not the Answer." *Managing Office Technology* (January 1996, vol. 41, no. 1), p. 30(3).

McNerney, Donald J. "The Cost of Loyalty Lost. Interview with Author Frederick F. Reichheld." *HR Focus* (June 1996, vol. 73, no. 6), p. 18(2).

Ruzow, Stephen L. "1996 Salary and Benefits for President and COO of Donna Karan International." *Daily News Record* (May 7, 1997, vol. 27, no. 55), p. 14(1).

"Salaries Are Going Up—If You're At the Right Firm." 1994 Contractor Management Salary & Benefits Survey. *Contractor* (July 1994, vol. 41, no. 7), p. 26(1).

Salisbury, Dallas L. "Benefit Planning and Management in a Changing Dynamic Labor Market." *Compensation and Benefits Review* (January/February 1997, vol. 29), p. 74(7).

Saltzman, Amy. "Little Conveniences That Make a Hit." *U.S. News & World Report* (January 16, 1995, vol. 118, no. 2), p. 62(2), Reference # A16003963.

Solomon, Charlene Marmer. "Testing at Odds with Diversity Efforts?" *Workforce* magazine, formerly known as *Personnel Journal* (April 1996, vol. 75, no. 4), p. 131(8).

Spragins, Ellyn E. "Reverse Reviews." *Inc.* (October 1992, vol. 14, no. 10), p. 33(1).

Truesdell, Martin. "Options Open When Picking Firm's Retirement Plan." Special Report: Taxes & Financial Planning. *Business First of Buffalo* (December 2, 1996, vol. 13, no. 8), p. 30(1).

Useem, Jerry. "Cutting Edge Benefits for Growing Companies." *Inc.* (February 1997, vol. 19, no. 2), p. S87(5).

Vogl, A.J. "A Black Hole? Benefits of Employer-Supported Employee Training." *Across the Board* (June 1996, vol. 33, no. 6), p. 1(1).

Voros, Sharon. "Managing Your Career: The New Realities." *Communication World* (February 1997, vol. 14, no. 3), p. 28(3).

———. "What Happens After the Interview?" *Financial Executive* (January/February 1997, vol. 13, no. 1), p. 24(3).

Troubleshooting: How to Respond When Employees Aren't Measuring Up

INTRODUCTION

It is quixotic to believe that it's possible in today's world to run a company of any size and not have to deal with employees who behave in ways that are not in the best interests of the company. Clearly, though, certain companies experience fewer such problems than others. Companies blessed with relatively few "people problems" obviously do a good job of recruiting and hiring good employees; smart hiring, after all, is the best way to avoid employee problems. And, as seen in previous chapters, successful companies generally have a culture that tends to breed satisfaction, not turmoil. But those companies that suffer the least from the most common people problems—absenteeism, tardiness, grievances, low morale, high turnover—also know how to respond when problems do arise. This chapter looks at some of the key practices that set these companies apart.

THE CHANGING ROLE OF SUPERVISION

One of the fundamental challenges in most companies today is shifting from traditional, hierarchy-based supervisory styles to the rapid pace and collaborative nature of today's workplace (see Table 10.1). Nearly everyone accepts the basic premise that the top-down, "command and control" approach to management does not foster the kind of innovation and commitment that companies need to remain competitive. But relatively few companies have figured out the best way to fill the void.

It is becoming more and more apparent, in fact, that one of the main reasons so many of the well-publicized initiatives over the past 10 years—self-directed teams, Total Quality Management (TQM), empowerment, and so forth—have failed in many companies is not because they were bad ideas, but because the line managers implementing them were unable to embrace the process or demonstrate the skills that were necessary to make the initiatives work.

As Philip Van Aucken, business consultant and management professor in the School of Business at Baylor University, has suggested, "Supervisors who are more concerned with controlling employees than developing them are simply out of step with today's marketplace realities. Controlled workers are poor team players, uncreative and very un-innovative."[1]

If anything can be learned from the experiences of the past 10 years as companies attempt to rein-

TABLE 10.1 THEN AND NOW: THE DIFFERENCE BETWEEN SUPERVISING AND COACHING

Traditional (supervisor)	Today (coach)
Giving orders	Seeking consensus
Control	Freedom
Insisting on obedience	Encouraging independent thinking
Rules and policies	Values and commitments
Telling people only what they need to know	Communicating openly
Focusing on results only	Paying attention to results and process

vent themselves, it is that none of the concepts or initiatives that have emerged over the past two decades is a "silver bullet." All take time and commitment. And, most importantly, initiatives designed to change the way companies operate need the support of employees throughout the organization, not just at the top.

APPRAISING PERFORMANCE: A FRESH LOOK AT AN OLD TOOL

Almost every company has some type of performance appraisal system that is used to make fundamental administrative decisions. These decisions typically include identifying which areas of performance need improvement, which employees should be promoted, and how much employees should be given in raises and bonuses. Performance appraisals have become increasingly important to companies that want to protect themselves from the spiraling number of wrongful dismissal suits. Such appraisals provide the documentation that helps companies defend themselves should the dismissal lead to arbitration or a court case.

Despite the widespread use of performance appraisals, however, one would be hard-pressed to find any company in which the managers responsible for administering the appraisals and the employees whose work is being evaluated are satisfied with the process. And no less an authority than the late Dr. D. W. Edwards Deming advocated, late in his career as a quality consultant, that performance appraisals be eliminated altogether. "Appraisal of people is ruinous," Deming argued in one of the last interviews he granted prior to his death in 1993 at the age of 93. "You cause humiliation, crush out joy of learning, innovation, joy on the job. Most of what anybody does is governed by the system that he works in. You are not evaluating him, you are evaluating the interaction with him and the system, the rules and constraints he works in."[2]

That judgment may be harsh, but it takes on a measure of legitimacy when one begins to consider the inherent pitfalls of the conventional performance appraisal methods, especially in today's workplace. Here, from a variety of sources, are the chief drawbacks of this familiar but often maligned management practice.

- The traditional approach to performance appraisal, with one supervisor passing judgment on the work of one or more direct reports, is antithetical to the spirit of openness and collaboration that many companies are trying to instill in their workplaces. Worse, the traditional one-to-one supervisory model has little or no relevance to managing self-directed teams.
- Traditional approaches to performance appraisals frequently place managers in a no-win situation: If managers give too favorable an appraisal, they run the risk of seeing a key employee get promoted to a better job in a different department. If, on the other hand, managers are brutally honest about the poor performance of too many employees whom they supervise, the bad ratings could increase turnover and cast a poor light on the manager's own supervisory skills.
- Even under the best of circumstances, performance appraisals almost always reflect subjective judgments. As such, appraisals work to the advantage of relatively mediocre employees who get along well with their supervisors and to the disadvantage of talented employees who don't get along with their supervisors. The process also creates inherent advantages for employees who work for lenient managers, and inherent disadvantages for those who work for demanding managers.
- Managers in most companies today are under excruciating time pressures and frequently do not give the appraisal process the time and attention it requires. A common complaint from employees in companies in which salaries are tied to performance ratings is that the rating process rarely takes place in a timely manner.

- Very few managers have been trained in the art of giving criticism. They often give undeservedly high ratings to relatively ineffective subordinates because they don't want to antagonize such employees.

Table 10.2 presents help for managers preparing for an appraisal session.

A NEW DIRECTION FOR AN OLD PRACTICE

Most companies are well aware of the performance appraisal problems just described, but few management specialists to date have been able to offer attractive alternatives. However, new approaches are beginning to appear.

Typifying the new approach to performance appraisals is the system developed in the early 1990s by Dow Chemical of North America. Convinced that its performance appraisal procedures were outdated, Dow decided in 1993 to replace its traditional system of appraisals. The company adopted an approach consistent with Deming's

TABLE 10.2 FIVE KEY QUESTIONS MANAGERS MUST ANSWER BEFORE BEGINNING AN APPRAISAL SESSION

Even when using traditional methods, there are ways that managers can avoid some of the problems commonly associated with performance appraisals and make better use of the appraisal process. Here are five key questions that any manager about to begin an appraisal should be prepared to answer.

1. Have I given the employee's performance enough time and thought to warrant a fair and objective appraisal?
2. Am I prepared to cite specific examples of strengths and weaknesses, and are they the best examples?
3. Have I thought about how this person accepts criticism, and am I able to adjust my delivery accordingly?
4. What has been the behavioral impact of previous performance appraisal sessions? Have they produced the expected and agreed-upon changes?
5. Has there been any fundamental change in the company or in the departmental activities that might account for a change in the employee's work performance?[3]

core principle that workers themselves must play a key role in the evaluation process. As Rebecca Walters, writing in *Business First—Columbus,* explained it, the central idea behind the Dow process is to have a supervisor and employee work together to decide what goals need to be accomplished and then determine what behavior will serve as evidence that the goal is being met.

Introducing this new system, of course, obliged Dow to eliminate many of the practices that characterized the older system, which was considered "demotivational" by nearly 80 percent of the workers. Raises, for instance, were no longer to be based on competitive evaluations, but on how well individual employees met the goals they themselves had been instrumental in setting. Gone, too, was the generic rating system that gave points for qualities such as "neatness" and "punctuality."[4]

THREE RULES OF THUMB FOR ESTABLISHING PERFORMANCE MEASURES

In any type of performance review, no factor is more important than the criteria that serve as the basis of the appraisal. Here are three guidelines well worth bearing in mind.

1. *Choose a manageable number:* Most consultants recommend strongly that managers show discipline and restraint when putting together the specific measurements to be used. Ideally, the number of criteria used in a performance appraisal should not exceed six.
2. *Balance financial and nonfinancial measurement:* The specific measurements eventually decided on should be both financial and nonfinancial. An example of financial measurement could be unit sales or some other aspect of productivity. A nonfinancial measurement might be the progress made toward a particular value that company is trying to foster, such as more open communication or enhanced teamwork.
3. *Be sensitive to improvement constraints.* Improvement constraints refer to the obstacles that stand in the way of performance gains in

any area. Most organizational development authorities consider that a moderate amount of constraint is desirable. But constraints should never be so severe that the gains in one measurement can be achieved only at the expense of others.[5]

THE SIX DEADLY SINS OF PERFORMANCE APPRAISALS

- *Haste:* Rushing through the process.
- *Bias:* Allowing personal biases and prejudices to have an impact on the process.
- *Avoidance:* Failing to address a problem in the hope that it will go away by itself.
- *Lack of preparation:* Failing to go into an appraisal session with all the facts in hand.
- *Insensitivity:* Failing to give enough thought to how people are likely to respond to criticism.
- *Lack of direction:* Using the appraisal as a "report card" and not a tool for improving performance or enhancing morale.[6]

MAKE APPRAISAL A TWO-WAY STREET

One of the ways that Datatec Industries, a New Jersey-based manufacturer of in-store computer systems with $32 million in annual revenues, decided to give some teeth to its empowerment initiatives was to reverse the appraisal process, allowing employees to grade their bosses.

The idea was introduced by the company's founder and president, Chris Carey, who started a long-range quality-improvement initiative in the early 1990s, but deliberately waited a few years before instituting the reverse appraisal process. Carey felt that such a process needed a culture that embodied values such as honesty, openness, empowerment, and acceptance of failure. The key instrument in the process is a 30-question form that each of the company's 318 employees is given an opportunity to fill out. Employees are asked to rate the company in four areas: morale, upper management, the employee's immediate manager, and the company's core values. Employees score their manager's skills in areas such as coaching, listening, praising, and responsiveness. Upper management is rated on its support of employees' articulation of goals, attentiveness to employee ideas, and fairness. To encourage employees to respond openly, Carey does not require that they sign their names to the surveys. Carey then gives managers a tally of the companywide responses and a similar tally of the answers given by their own subordinates.[7]

NO MORE MR. NICE GUY

DANGER!

Managers who show too much leniency when conducting performance appraisals could be inadvertently exposing their companies to wrongful dismissal suits if it ever becomes necessary to dismiss an employee for poor performance. The reason: employees in wrongful dismissal suits frequently use positive performance appraisals (accurate or not) to "prove" that the company dismissed them for reasons other than performance.

KEY CONCEPT

PROGRESSIVE DISCIPLINE

There are differing views on whether or not progressive discipline is an effective staffing practice. The process involves creating a series of stages that give an employee the opportunity to correct poor performance, but culminate in dismissal if the problem persists. However, many companies believe that this approach restricts their ability to take swift action when appropriate, and that it may in fact create additional legal exposure, if the progressive discipline process is not followed in every situation. These companies prefer the flexibility of responding according to the individual circumstances.

FOLLOW THE HOT STOVE RULE WHEN APPLYING DISCIPLINE

Many companies, in an attempt to simplify and bring consistency to their dismissal policies, follow what has come to be known as the "hot stove rule." The moving force behind the rule is that discipline should always be directed against the *behavior* and not the person. Here are the three key principles of the rule.

1. *Immediacy:* Discipline should always be administered as quickly as is appropriate under the circumstances. (A hot stove burns immediately.)
2. *Warning:* Discipline should, if appropriate, include some sort of warning. (A hot stove usually has smoke.)
3. *Consistent and impartial:* Discipline should be consistent. (A hot stove causes the same burn to everyone who touches it.)[8]

DEALING WITH SUBSTANCE ABUSE

Substance abuse is a problem most companies are reluctant to talk about, even though it is generally conceded that as much as 15 percent of the American workforce is under the influence of either alcohol or some other drug on any given day.[9]

To be sure, there is no easy solution to the substance abuse problem in today's workplace, and the issues at the core of the problem are as much a function of social issues as workplace pressures. Even so, there are certain steps companies can take to keep substance abuse problems under reasonable control.

- *Establish a written policy on substance abuse:* A written policy on substance use and abuse should be an essential ingredient in any company's policy and procedures manual. Care should be taken to ensure that the policy is legal, and there should be a clear statement of the consequences in the event employees are under the influence of drugs while on company time or are possessing, selling, or distributing illegal substances.
- *Train managers to recognize the signs of substance abuse:* Managers should be trained to recognize employees who may be having a sub-

stance abuse problem. The most common symptoms are a sudden and unexplained increase in absenteeism or tardiness, and noticeable—and unexplainable—differences in workplace behavior. See Table 10.3 for a complete list of signs.

- *Consider establishing an employee assistance program (EAP):* Many major American companies offer programs or access to programs designed to help employees deal with substance abuse problems. The key success ingredient in these programs is confidentiality. Employees need to be assured that by admitting to a problem and enrolling in a program, they will not be jeopardizing their jobs or their chances for advancement.
- *Practice early intervention:* The sooner a substance abuse problem is identified, the easier it is to deal with and solve.
- *Launch an education program:* The effectiveness of any drug or alcohol abuse education program in the workplace has yet to be established, but companies that have launched such programs seem happy with the results. Burlington Northern Santa Fe hands out free T-shirts and caps with slogans such as "Drugs and Alcohol Don't Work Here." As one company spokesman explained it, "The real strength of our prevention program is not so much the intervention piece (getting employees the help

TABLE 10.3 SUBSTANCE ABUSE: THE SIGNS

- Increased absenteeism and tardiness, especially on Mondays and Fridays, and before and after holidays
- Frequent unreported "emergencies"
- Frequent colds, flu viruses, upset stomachs, headaches, and so on
- Higher than average accident rates on and off the job
- A depressed or anxious disposition
- A tendency to overreact to real or imagined criticism
- A tendency to be overly withdrawn or improperly talkative[10]

they need); it's more the visibility in the workplace of the message that substance abuse is unacceptable."[11]

- *Keep careful records:* Managers should carefully document the performance of substance abusers so that they can assess the success of intervention and make a case for termination, if necessary.

HOW TO STAY OUT OF HARM'S WAY ON THE FIRING ISSUE

The most direct way of dealing with an employee whose job performance is not measuring up to standards or is causing problems is to dismiss the employee. Even the most people-oriented companies recognize that in many instances firing represents the only solution. The need to fire, however, is complicated these days by any number of factors, quite apart from the psychological and financial impact it has on the person who is being let go.

- The supply of qualified replacements in some industries and in some parts of the country is so limited that it could well take an unacceptably long time to find someone.
- Despite the fact that employment at will still applies in most states, companies are more vulnerable than ever to wrongful dismissal suits, especially when the dismissed employee falls into any of the categories protected by federal, state, or local laws.
- The havoc that can be wreaked on a company by disgruntled ex-employees who believe they have been unfairly treated has been magnified in recent years, because so much of a company's assets is in the form of intellectual property that can be easily stolen or sabotaged.
- Even when it is justified, an employee dismissal has a major impact on the morale and the productivity of coworkers. Incompetent employees are not necessarily unpopular employees. And the need to pick up the slack until the replacement is found can often breed resentment.

WHY *NOT* FIRING CAN BE DANGEROUS

DANGER!

Faced with the growing threat of wrongful dismissal lawsuits, managers in many companies today have become understandably reluctant to dismiss employees who are underperforming or creating problems. But there is a danger to this seemingly conservative approach to dismissal. Writing in *HR Magazine,* Jonathan Segal suggests that employers who fail to take action when the presence of a problem employee endangers the well-being of other employees could risk legal action from anyone who becomes a victim of the problem employee's incompetence or violent acts.[12]

PREVENTIVE ACTION: FIVE WAYS TO CONTROL DISMISSAL PROBLEMS

1. *Adopt more rigorous hiring policies:* It is not by coincidence that the companies that enjoy the lowest rates of turnover in their respective industries are usually those that are the most rigorous in their hiring policies. So the first thing a company being bedeviled by unusually high turnover rates needs to do is take a second look at how and why so many people who don't work out are being hired in the first place. Following are some of the specific things to look at.
2. *Make orientation meaningful:* Paying more attention to how effective new employee orientations are can make a difference in turnover in a number of ways. For one thing, effective orientation policies go a long way in preventing many of the adjustment problems that often lie at the core of most dismissals. Relationships get off to a better start; expectations are more clearly understood. Equally important, when orientation is combined with training, it functions in effect as a "probation period." Employees who are clearly ill-suited to the culture often leave on their own accord.
3. *Be wary of implicit guarantees of employment:* It is essential in today's litigious environment

that companies review their recruiting literature and manuals to make sure that there are neither explicit nor implicit assurances of job security. Supervisors, too, must be cautioned against making commitments and promises that could be construed as an implicit guarantee of employment and could leave the company open to a lawsuit.

4. *Learn from mistakes:* High levels of turnover can often be traced to inefficient and slapdash hiring practices. Companies experiencing high turnover would do well to reexamine their hiring criteria and procedures and make sure that the hiring process is being carried out in a disciplined, well-thought-out manner that is keyed to strategic objectives of the business and that acknowledges realities of the local labor market.
5. *Be sensitive to the reaction of other workers:* Even when the firing is clearly justified, managers should be sensitive to the reactions of other department members. Any employee dismissal has a major impact on the morale and the productivity of coworkers. It is therefore important that managers recognize in advance the repercussions that may occur.

ESTABLISH A FAIR AND CONSISTENT SEVERANCE POLICY

It has not yet been established that generous severance policies significantly reduce a company's chances of being sued for wrongful dismissal, but common sense says that the fairer and more generous a company is with the people it has to let go, the less likely it is that the employees will cause problems. Severance policies vary widely from company to company and from industry to industry. In general, though, the amount of severance (when not determined by a contract) is based on three factors: salary, length of time in service, and company practices.

Most companies are reluctant to share their severance policies with the outside world, but a report in *HR Magazine* sheds some light on how one corporate giant, AT&T, has handled severance payments throughout the 1990s.[13]

AT&T's aim, according to George A. Fromme, the company's vice president for benefits planning, health insurance and quality measurements, is to provide affected employees with "a soft landing." As *HR Magazine* reported, AT&T's normal severance package is based primarily on the number of years the employee has been with the company (one week for each year), but it also takes into account the age of the employee (older employees are given a more generous package) and includes supplemental severance for employees who agree to voluntary termination.

It should be pointed out that unless there are specific contractual obligations, companies are under no obligation to provide any severance whatsoever. The decision, in the end, comes down to what the company deems is "fair." The AT&T example demonstrates some of the factors that companies might want to consider when setting up their own policies.

END POINT

The same combination of competitive pressures and social trends that has created the need for new approaches to hiring has created a corresponding need for changes in the way employees are managed. Performance appraisals, discipline, and terminations are just a few of the areas in which management practices have had to adapt.

As pointed out early in the chapter, one of the ongoing challenges facing employers in every industry is the transition from the hierarchical, top-down style of supervision to a more collaborative style in which managers function more as coaches than they do as supervisors. One aspect of this challenge has been to develop ways of evaluating performance in a team-based environment. Giving employees more direct involvement in the appraisal process is yet another related development.

Companies are also taking a much more proactive approach to keeping turnover to a manageable minimum and to dealing with such growing problems as substance abuse. Finally, given the upsurge in the number of wrongful dismissal suits that have been filed in recent years, progressive companies have been scrutinizing their termination policies more carefully and have been taking an increasingly proactive approach to controlling turnover.

MORE READING

"Bright Tomorrows." *Human Resource Executive* (October 3, 1996).

Crispell, Diane. "How to Manage a Chaotic Workplace." *American Demographics* (June 1996).

Johnson, Kirk. "In Changed Landscape of Recruiting, Academic and Corporate Worlds Merge." *New York Times* (December 4, 1996).

Michal-Johnson, Paula. *Saying Good-Bye: A Manager's Guide to Employee Dismissal.* Glenview, Illinois: Scott, Foresman and Company, 1985.

Mogelonsky, Marcia. "Happy Workers, Lower Costs." *American Demographics* (July 1994).

Nilson, Carolyn. *Training for Non-Trainers: A Do-It-Yourself Guide for Managers.* New York: Amacom, 1990.

Spragins, Ellyn E. "Reverse Reviews." *Inc.* (October, 1992, vol. 14, no. 10), p. 33(1).

Walton, Mary. *Deming Management At Work.* New York: G. P. Putnam's Sons, 1990.

Wendover, Robert W. *Smart Hiring For Your Business: The Complete Guide to Finding and Hiring the Best Employees.* Naperville, Illinois: Sourcebooks Trade, 1993.

Woodward, Harry and Steve Buchholz. *AFTERSHOCK: Helping People Through Corporate Change.* New York: John Wiley & Sons, 1987.

APPENDIX

HELPFUL HR WEB SITES

The following Web sites are full of useful and current information.

1. Society for Human Resource Management: http://www.shrm.org/
   - SHRM's Web site is full of HR resources, including *HR Magazine* on-line, and regional and worldwide conference information. This site also provides links to other helpful HR Web sites.
2. Gateway to Internet resources for HR staff: http://www.teleport.com/~erwilson/
   - This site consists of a large collection of HR-related Web sites that may be accessed by clicking on the Web site's name. A description is included with each site. This gateway is maintained by HR Integrated Solutions, Inc.

ON-LINE MAGAZINES

The following on-line magazines have pertinent articles and a database of archived HR material.

1. *HR Magazine:* http://www.shrm.org/hrmagazine/articles/0796w95a.htm
2. *Fast Company:* http://www.fastcompany.com/
3. *Workforce:* http://www.workforceonline.com

GOVERNMENT WEB SITES

For up-to-date statistics, reports, and information on changes in work-related policies, these Web sites have the most recent information.

1. Bureau of Labor:
   http://stats.bls.gov/
   - This site provides general data, regional info, and links to other statistical sites.
2. Internet Legal Resources:
   http://www.findlaw.com/
   - The legal resources site contains information on United States federal laws and regulations, as well as additional legal resources.
3. Gateway to all United States federal government agencies:
   http://www.lib.1su.edu/gov/fedgov.html
   - This site provides easy access to the executive, judicial, and legislative branches of the federal government.
4. Department of Labor:
   http://www.dolgov/
   - Access this site to find information on labor-related subjects such as minimum wage standards, statutory and regulatory information, labor-related data, and compliance information and assistance.

DEPENDENT CARE BENEFIT RESOURCES INFORMATION

The Dependent Care Connection, Inc. (DCC)

P.O. Box 2783
Westport, CT 06880
Phone: 203-226-2680
Fax: 203-226-2852
Website: dccwebmaster@dcclifecare.com

Work/Family Direction, Inc.

930 Commonwealth Avenue
Boston, MA 02215
Phone: 617-278-4000

POTENTIAL EMPLOYEE BENEFITS, LISTED IN ORDER OF MOST FREQUENTLY TO LEAST FREQUENTLY OFFERED

Paid leave

Employer-paid jury duty
Time off for death in the family
Sick time
10+ holidays
Personal days
National Guard duty

Insurance

Group health
Group life
Long-term disability
Short-term disability

Bonus/Pension/Thrift

401(k)
Pension
Holiday/year-end bonus
Profit sharing

Miscellaneous

Mileage allowance
Shift premium
Cafeteria plan
Employee Assistance Plans
Flexible work hours
Exempt overtime
Birthday off
Business and professional memberships
Company-provided equipment (cars, computers, office supplies, etc.)
On-site child care, or child care allowance

Note: Certain benefits listed above may be required by collective bargaining agreements or by state or federal law.

Sick child care allowance
Time off for educational activities
Stipend toward continuing education
Subsidized meals
Interest-free loans
Legal assistance
Matching educational donations
Personal credit cards
Recreation facilities
Stock purchase plans

STANDARD HOLIDAYS

These are the standard holiday closings for most businesses.

New Year's Day
Memorial Day
Labor Day
Fourth of July
Thanksgiving
Christmas

These are the next most popular holiday closings.

Friday after Thanksgiving
Washington's Birthday
Good Friday[1]

SPECIALTY REWARD ITEMS FOR EMPLOYEES

American Express Corporate Sales

100 Church Street, 14th Floor
New York, NY 10007-1400
800-666-7317
Gift cheques that the employee can use almost anywhere

Wonton Food Inc.

Fortune Cookie Division
220–222 Moore Street
Brooklyn, NY 11206
718-628-6868
Fortune cookies with personalized messages

Harry and David

2518 S. Pacific Hwy.
Medford, OR 97501
800-248-5567
Gift baskets of fresh fruits, meats, seafood

Hillerich & Bradsby Company

Premium and Incentive Dept.
P.O. Box 35700
Louisville, KY 40232
502-585-5226 or 800-282-2287
Sporting equipment with customized imprinting

John's Inc.

800 W. Johns Road
Apopka, FL 32703
407-886-8850
Live potted plants that can be customized with name of company or individual

Lalique Crystal

Special Markets Division
41 Madison Avenue
New York, NY 10010
212-684-6338
Crystal objects that can be customized

LTD Commodities, Inc.

2800 Lakeside Drive
Bannockburn, IL 60015
847-295-6058
Catalog of gifts and collectibles

Parker Pen U.S.A. Ltd.

1400 N. Parker Drive
Janesville, WI 53545
608-755-7000 or 800-522-3021
Pens that may be personalized with company logo or individual's name

Sweet Nut Tree

43 S. Huron Street
Toledo, OH 43602
800-477-6887
Gourmet nuts and candies in jars or tins that can be customized with name/logo

Swiss Army Brand, Inc.

1 Research Drive
P.O. Box 874
Shelton, CT 06484-0874
800-243-4032
A variety of knives, watches, and other useful items that can be engraved

Tiffany & Co.

727 Fifth Avenue
New York, NY 10022
212-735-0035 or 800-423-2394
Custom-engraved silver gifts

NOTES

CHAPTER 1

1. William Bridges, *JobShift: How to Prosper in a Workplace Without Jobs* (Reading, MA: Addison-Wesley, 1995), p. 30.
2. Human Resource Financial Report, Saratoga Institute, *Staffing Industry Report* (July 1997). Figure refers to hiring costs in 1996.
3. Frederick F. Reichheld, Director of Bain & Company, *The Loyalty Effect* (Boston: Harvard Business School Press, 1996), p. 45.
4. Robert Lenzner and Stephen S. Johnson, "Still the Youngest Mind," *Forbes* (March 3, 1997).
5. Amanda Bennett, *Death of The Organization Man* (New York: William Morrow & Company, 1990), p. 51.
6. Lenzner and Johnson.
7. Farah M. Walters, "Successfully Managing Diversity: Why the Right Thing to Do Is Also the Smart Thing to Do," *Vital Speeches* (June 1995).
8. U.S. Department of Census, 1995.
9. Kerry Dolan, "When Money Isn't Enough," *Forbes* (November 1996).
10. Ibid.

CHAPTER 2

1. Author interview.
2. David D. Jones, "Repositioning Human Resources: A Case Study," *Human Resource*

Planning (March 1996), pp. 51–53. Reprinted by permission of the Human Resource Planning Society, 317 Madison Avenue, Suite 1509, New York, NY 10017, Phone: (212) 490-6387, Fax: (212) 682-6851.

3. A. J. Vogl, "Growing Pains," *Across the Board* (February 1997), p. 43.
4. Thomas P. Bechet and James W. Walker, "Aligning Staffing with Business Strategy," *Human Resource Planning* (June 1993), p. 1. Reprinted by permission of the Human Resource Planning Society, 317 Madison Avenue, Suite 1509, New York, NY 10017, Phone: (212) 490-6387, Fax: (212) 682-6851
5. Milan Moravec and Robert Tucker, "Job Descriptions for the 21st Century," *Personnel Journal* (currently known as *Workforce*) (June 1992), p. 37.
6. Susan R. Duncan, "Be Realistic: Job Previews are Tied to Survival Rates," *Managers Magazine* (November 1994), p. 15.
7. Peter Carbona, "Hire for Attitude, Train for Skill," *Fast Company* (August/September 1996), p. 73.
8. Author interview.
9. Ellyn E. Spragins, "Hiring Without The Guesswork," adapted with permission, *Inc.* (February 1992), p. 33. Copyright 1992 by Goldhirsh Group, Inc., 38 Commercial Wharf, Boston, MA 02110.

CHAPTER 3

1. Shari Caudron, "Contingent Workforce Spurs HR Planning," *Personnel Journal* (currently known as *Workforce*) (July 1994), pp. 52–58.
2. Dawn Anfuso, "Staffing System Gives 3M Growth and Stability," *Personnel Journal* (currently known as *Workforce*) (January 1995), p. 80.
3. Shari Caudron.
4. Bob Nelson, "The Care of the Un-Downsized," *Training & Development* (April 1997), pp. 40–43.

5. Frederick F. Reichheld, Director of Bain & Company, *The Loyalty Effect* (Boston: Harvard Business School Press, 1996), p. 81.
6. Michael Hammer and James Champy, *Reengineering the Corporation: A Manifesto for Business Revolution* (New York: Harper Business, 1993), p. 95.
7. Shari Caudron.
8. Julie Mason, "A Temp-ting Staffing Strategy," *Management Review* (February 1996), p. 33.
9. Author interview, NATSS.
10. Gillian Flynn, "Contingent Staffing Requires Serious Strategy," *Personnel Journal* (currently known as *Workforce*) (April 1995), pp. 50–55.
11. Author interview.
12. Author interview.
13. Gifford and Elizabeth Pinchot, *The Intelligent Organization* (New York: Berret-Koehler Publications, 1995), p. 155.
14. T. Joe Willey, *Directory of PEOs,* Staffing Industry Resources (1997), and the National Association of Professional Employer Organizations.
15. Dawn Anfuso, "Staffing System Gives 3M Growth and Stability," *Personnel Journal* (currently known as *Workforce*) (January 1995), p. 80.

CHAPTER 4

1. Rom Zemke and Rick Schaff, *The Service Edge* (New York: NAL Books, 1989), p. 180.
2. Ibid., p. 192.
3. Frederick F. Reichheld, Director of Bain & Company, *The Loyalty Effect* (Boston: Harvard Business School Press, 1996), p. 148.
4. Ibid.
5. Ibid.
6. Donna Fenn, "Bottoms Up Best Advancement Award," adapted with permission, *Inc.* (July 1993). Copyright 1993 by Goldhirsch Group, Inc., 38 Commercial Wharf, Boston, MA 02110.
7. Dennis Guessford, Albert B. Boynton, Robert Laudeman Jr., and Joseph P. Grusti, "Tracing

Job Skills Improves Performance," *Personnel Journal* (currently known as *Workforce*) (June 1993), pp. 109–114.

8. "Bring Your Friends to Work," adapted with permission, *Inc.* (November 1988), p. 149. Copyright 1988 by Goldhirsh Group, Inc., 38 Commercial Wharf, Boston, MA 02110.
9. Gene Paul, "Talent Pool: Hiring is All in the Family," *Fast Company* (August/September 1996), p. 81.
10. Karen E. Carney, "Tough Love," adapted with permission, *Inc.* (September 1994). Copyright 1994 by Goldhirsch Group, Inc., 38 Commercial Wharf, Boston, MA 02110.
11. Reichheld, p. 93.
12. Ellyn E. Spragins, "Hiring Without the Guesswork," adapted with permission, *Inc.* (February 1992). Copyright 1992 by Goldhirsh Group, Inc., 38 Commercial Wharf, Boston, MA 02110.
13. Donna Fenn, "How to Write an Ad," adapted with permission, *Inc.* (May 1989). Copyright 1989 by Goldhirsh Group, Inc., 38 Commercial Wharf, Boston, MA 02110.
14. *NetMarketing Web Price Index* (Crain Communications, April 1997), http://www.netb2b.com
15. Sara Selis, "Online Job Recruiting Turns Up Best and Brightest at Low Cost," *Business First—Columbus* (September 1996), pp. 17–18.
16. Michael P. Cronin, "Co-op Student Internships," adapted with permission, *Inc.* (April 1993). Copyright 1993 by Goldhirsh Group, Inc., 38 Commercial Wharf, Boston, MA 02110.
17. Ibid.
18. "Creative Staffing Drives Success," *Personnel Journal* (currently known as *Workforce*) (March 1996).

CHAPTER 5

1. Peter Carbonara, "Hire for Attitude, Train for Skill," *Fast Company* (August/September 1996), p. 71.
2. Ibid.

3. Tom Peters, *Thriving on Chaos* (Alfred Knopf, 1987), p. 30.
4. "Read Between the Lines, Managing People," adapted with permission, *Inc.* (June 1995). Copyright 1995 by Goldhirsh Group, Inc., 38 Commercial Wharf, Boston, MA 02110.
5. "How to Write an Ad," adapted with permission, *Inc.* (May 1989). Copyright 1989 by Goldhirsh Group, Inc., 38 Commercial Wharf, Boston, MA 02110.
6. "Best Practices: Hiring," adapted with permission, *Inc.* (March 1994). Copyright 1994 by Goldhirsh Group, Inc., 38 Commercial Wharf, Boston, MA 02110. pp.

CHAPTER 6

1. Tom Peters, *Thriving on Chaos* (Alfred Knopf, 1987), p. 48.
2. "Old Interview Methods Proving Ineffective," *USA Today Magazine* (December 8, 1996).
3. Ibid.
4. Author interview.
5. Author interview.
6. John Drake, *Interviewing for Managers* (New York: AMACOM, 1982), p. 160.
7. Eliott Aronson, *The Social Animal* (New York: W. H. Freeman & Company, 1965), p. 174.
8. John B. Holderman, Jeffrey M. Aldridge, and David Jackson, "How to Hire Ms./Mr. Right," *Journal of Accountancy* (August 1996), pp. 55–57.

CHAPTER 7

1. Author interview.
2. Lloyd L. Byars and Leslie W. Rue, *Human Resource Management,* 5th ed. (Chicago: McGraw-Hill, 1997), p. 38.
3. Charlene M. Solomon, "Testing at Odds With Diversity Efforts?" *Personnel Journal* (currently known as *Workforce*) (April 1996), p. 42.
4. Ibid.

5. "Pre-employment Testing Programs," *Supervision* (October 1995), pp. 17–18.
6. Solomon, pp. 131–138.
7. Donna Fenn, "Employee Auditions," adapted with permission, *Inc. Magazine* (June 1996). Copyright 1996 by Goldhirsh Group, Inc., Boston, MA 02110.
8. Robert Lavigna, "Innovation in Recruiting and Hiring: Attracting the Best and Brightest to Wisconsin State Government," *Public Personnel Management* (Winter 1996).
9. Daniel Seligman, "Searching for Integrity," *Fortune* (March 1993).
10. Byars and Rue, p. 64.
11. Geoffrey Brewer, "Shrink Rap: Is It Smart—Or Just Plain Crazy—To Use Psychological Tests When Hiring and Developing Employees?" *Sales & Marketing Management* (September 1995), pp. 28–32.
12. Mary LeBone, "Testing Hair for Illicit Drug Use" *National Institute of Justice Research Brief* (January 1993).
13. Peter Carbonara, "The Secrets of Their Success," *Fast Company* (June 1997), p. 67.
14. Philip E. Ross, "They Play to Win," *Forbes* (March 13, 1995), pp. 162–163.

CHAPTER 8

1. Michael Losey, "Reference-Checking Protocols Leave Everyone in the Dark," *Managing Office Technology* (November 1995), p. 33.
2. Bill Leonard, "Reference-Checking Laws: Now What?" *HR Magazine* (December 1995), pp. 57–60.
3. Ibid.
4. Ibid.
5. "Reference Checking Gets Creative," *Personnel Journal* (currently known as *Workforce*) (August 1994), pp. 22–23.
6. Leonard, pp. 57–60.
7. John D. Drake, *Interviewing for Managers* (New York: AMACON, 1982), p. 140.

8. Author interview.
9. "Negotiating Employment Agreements," *Management Review* (January 1997), p. 62.

CHAPTER 9

1. Mark A. Huselid, "The Impact of Human Resource Management Practices on Turnover, Productivity, and Corporate Financial Performance," citation: *Academy of Management Journal* (June 1995).
2. Ronald Henkoff, "Finding, Training and Keeping the Best Service Workers," *Fortune* (October 3, 1994).
3. Ibid.
4. Karen Bridges, Gail Hawkins, and Kelli Elledge, "From New Recruit to Team Member," *Training & Development* (August 1993), p. 55.
5. Carol S. Klein and Jeff Taylor, "Employee Orientation is an Ongoing Process at the DuPont Merck Pharmaceutical Co.," *Personnel Journal* (currently known as *Workforce*) (May 1994), p. 67.
6. Cheri A. Young and Craig C. Lundberg, "Creating a Good First Day on the Job; Allaying Newcomers' Anxiety with Positive Messages," *Cornell Hotel & Restaurant Administration Quarterly* (December 1996), p. 26.
7. Alice M. Starcke, "Building a Better Orientation Program," *HR Magazine* (November 1996), pp. 107–112.
8. Ibid.
9. Young and Lundberg.
10. Starcke.
11. "How to Interview, Hire, and Bring New Employees on Board," *Supervisory Management* (May 1994), p. 7.
12. Jennifer J. Laabs, "Embrace Today's New Deal," *Workforce* (August 1996).
13. "What Labor Shortage?" *Fortune Magazine* (June 23, 1997).
14. Author interview.
15. Frederick F. Reichheld, Director of Bain & Company, *The Loyalty Effect* (Harvard Business School Press, 1996), p. 86.

16. Lloyd L. Byars and Leslie W. Rue, *Human Resource Management,* 5th ed. (Chicago: McGraw-Hill, 1997), p. 292.

17. D. L. Kirkpatrick, "Evaluation of Training," *Training and Development Handbook* (New York: McGraw-Hill, 1986), p. 81.

18. Amy Saltzman, "Companies in a Family Way," *U.S. News & World Report* (May 12, 1997), pp. 64–67.

19. Keith Hammonds, "Balancing Work and Family," *Business Week* (September 9, 1996).

20. Saltzman.

21. Hammonds

22. Kerry Dolan, When Money Isn't Enough, *Forbes Magazine* (November 1996).

23. Hammonds

24. Author interview.

25. Dolan.

26. *The Dependent Care Connection,* United HealthCare, press release (January 1, 1997).

27. Hammonds.

28. Dolan.

29. Sherri Merl and Gerald E. Connally, "Telecommuting: Evolution or Revolution," *Solutions* (February 1996).

30. Hammonds.

31. Donald Dann, "Nurturing Workers so They'll Stay on Board," reprinted by permission, *Nation's Business* (August 1996), p. 6. Copyright 1996, U.S. Chamber of Commerce.

32. Ibid.

33. Hammonds.

34. Yuan Ting, "Analysis of Job Satisfaction of the Federal White-Collar Work Force: Findings from the Survey of Federal Employees," *American Review of Public Administration* (December 1996).

CHAPTER 10

1. Philip M. Van Auken, "Control vs. Development: Up-To-Date as a Supervisor?" *Supervision* (December 1992), pp. 17–19.

2. Tim Stevens, "Dr. Deming: Management Today Does Not Know What Its Job Is," *Industry Week* (January 17, 1994), pp. 20–24.
3. Ted Pollock, "Ready for That Appraisal?" *Supervision* (February 1995), pp. 24–26.
4. Rebecca Walters, "Employee Evaluation is Different at Dow," *Business First—Columbus* (May 1993), p. 4.
5. Lloyd L. Byars and Leslie W. Rue, *Human Resource Management,* Fifth Edition (Chicago: McGraw-Hill Books, 1997), p. 469.
6. Pollock.
7. Ellyn E. Spragins, "Hiring Without the Guesswork," adapted with permission, *Inc.* magazine (October 1992) p. 33. Copyright 1992 by Goldhirsh Group, Inc., 38 Commercial Wharf, Boston, MA 02110.
8. Byars and Rue.
9. Robert H. Rosen, Ph.D. with Lisa Berger, *The Healthy Company* (New York: G. P. Putnam's Sons, 1991), p. 174.
10. Ceridian Employee Advisory Resource. Center for Substance Abuse Prevention Workplace Hotline: 800-843-4971.
11. "Substance Abuse in the Workplace," *HR Focus* (February 1997), pp. 1–3.
12. Jonathan A. Segal, "When Norman Bates and Baby June Act Out at Work," *HR Magazine* (February 1996), pp. 31–35.
13. Joan Szabo, "Severance Plans Shift Away From Cash," *HR Magazine* (July 1996), pp. 104–106.

APPENDIX

1. Author interview, Chris Persson, Personnel Management Services, Stratford, CT 06497.

CREDITS

David D. Jones, "Repositioning Human Resources: A Case Study," pp. 51–53. Reprinted with permission from *Human Resource Planning* (March 1996), by the Human Resource Planning Society, 317 Madison Avenue, Suite 1509, New York, NY 10017, phone (212) 490-6387, fax (212) 682-6851.

Thomas P. Bechet and James W. Walker, "Aligning Staffing with Business Strategy," p. 1. Reprinted with permission from *Human Resource Planning* (June 1993), by the Human Resource Planning Society, 317 Madison Avenue, Suite 1509, New York, NY 10017, phone (212) 490-6387, fax (212) 682-6851.

Ellyn E. Spragins, "Hiring without the Guesswork," adapted with permission, *Inc.* magazine (February 1992), p. 33. Copyright 1992 by Goldhirsh Group, Inc., 38 Commercial Wharf, Boston, MA 02110.

Donna Fenn, "Bottoms Up Best Advancement Award," adapted with permission, *Inc.* magazine (July 1993). Copyright 1993 by Goldhirsch Group, Inc., 38 Commercial Wharf, Boston, MA 02110.

"Bring Your Friends to Work," adapted with permission, *Inc.* magazine (November 1988), p. 149. Copyright 1988 by Goldhirsh Group, Inc., 38 Commercial Wharf, Boston, MA 02110.

Karen E. Carney, "Tough Love," adapted with permission, *Inc.* magazine (September 1994).

Copyright 1994 by Goldhirsch Group, Inc., 38 Commercial Wharf, Boston, MA 02110.

"How to Write an Ad," adapted with permission, *Inc.* magazine (May 1989). Copyright 1989 by Goldhirsh Group, Inc., 38 Commercial Wharf, Boston, MA 02110.

Michael P. Cronin, "Co-op Student Internships," adapted with permission, *Inc.* magazine (April 1993). Copyright 1993 by Goldhirsh Group, Inc., 38 Commercial Wharf, Boston, MA 02110.

Donna Fenn, "Searching for the Chosen Few," adapted with permission, *Inc.* magazine (March 1996). Copyright 1996 by Goldhirsh Group, Inc., 38 Commercial Wharf, Boston, MA 02110.

"Read Between the Lines, Managing People," adapted with permission, *Inc.* magazine (June 1995). Copyright 1995 by Goldhirsh Group, Inc., 38 Commercial Wharf, Boston, MA 02110.

"Best Practices—Hiring," adapted with permission, *Inc.* magazine (March 1994). Copyright 1994 by Goldhirsh Group, Inc., 38 Commercial Wharf, Boston, MA 02110.

"Employee Auditions," adapted with permission, *Inc.* magazine (June 1996). Copyright 1996 by Goldhirsh Group, Inc., Boston, MA 02110.

Donald Dann, "Nurturing Workers So They'll Stay On Board," reprinted by permission, *Nation's Business* (August 1996), p. 6. Copyright 1996, U.S. Chamber of Commerce.

Florence Stone, "How to Interview, Hire and Bring New Employees On Board," reprinted by permission of the publisher, from *Supervisory Management* (May 1994). Copyright 1994 by American Management Association, New York. All rights reserved.

Keith Hammonds, "Balancing Work and Family," (September 16, 1996), by permission of *Business Week,* Copyright 1997.

INDEX